SEEKING THE GIFT OF GOOD FORTUNE

Legends and Myths
of the I Ching and the Time Before Time

A Brief Introduction to Taoism, Divination
And the Mysteries of That Which Always Is

ROSE ROYSE

BALBOA.PRESS
A DIVISION OF HAY HOUSE

Balboa Press books may be ordered through booksellers or by contacting:

Balboa Press
A Division of Hay House
1663 Liberty Drive
Bloomington, IN 47403
www.balboapress.com
844-682-1282

Because of the dynamic nature of the Internet, any web addresses or
links contained in this book may have changed since publication and
may no longer be valid. The views expressed in this work are solely those
of the author and do not necessarily reflect the views of the publisher,
and the publisher hereby disclaims any responsibility for them.

The author of this book does not dispense medical advice or prescribe the use
of any technique as a form of treatment for physical, emotional, or medical
problems without the advice of a physician, either directly or indirectly. The
intent of the author is only to offer information of a general nature to help
you in your quest for emotional and spiritual well-being. In the event you use
any of the information in this book for yourself, which is your constitutional
right, the author and the publisher assume no responsibility for your actions.

Any people depicted in stock imagery provided by Getty Images are
models, and such images are being used for illustrative purposes only.
Certain stock imagery © Getty Images.

Print information available on the last page.

ISBN: 979-8-7652-3099-2 (sc)
ISBN: 979-8-7652-3100-5 (e)

Balboa Press rev. date: 08/26/2022

The Gift of Good Fortune

A Journal for the Awakening of Self-Awareness

Seeking good fortune she went to the gift shop,
certain that there would be good fortune,
wrapped in a gift box for a reasonable price.

She was astonished to discover,
while talking with the clerk, that good fortune was free,
however, to receive it in a gift box was quite costly.

There was a way to earn the cost of the gift wrapping.
She was instructed to step into the sanctuary
behind the curtain, to gain access to the gift.

Looking around, making certain that her friends
did not notice, she stepped through the curtain.

The voice of the Oracle said
"Welcome, come on in, how can we help you?"

Shyly she requested the gift of good fortune.

Feeling herself rising above the earth,
like in a beautiful dream, she saw the gift.

She reached out, hoping to hold it in her hand,
only to discover that as she reached for the gift,
she found herself entranced at the doorway of
"That Which Always Is".

Good fortune is inspired by the story you tell yourself.

About the Author
A Story Yet to be Told

There was a time when I planted some seeds,
to grow new crops.

As time passed, I waited,
seeing nothing emerging from below.

I grew impatient, and tried to help the seeds,
by removing some of the dirt.

Hastily I worked to make it easier for the seedlings
to reach the light.

The seedlings that I helped withered and died,
exposed before their time.

Those that I did not help emerged as a healthy harvest.

With new awareness, I do not hasten to influence.
I engage in new beginnings only when the time is right.

I stand before you now,
with a peek into the secrets,
of the gift of good fortune.

The stories herein provide guidance
for the contemplation of your everyday concerns.

Step forward now, resolving your concerns
into the self-realization of harmony within.
Embrace the balance of Yin and Yang.

That Which Always Is

Seeking

To Inquire, to Quest, to Search

The I Ching is one of the oldest written histories
of the evolution and migrations of humanity. The I
Ching enlightens, offering a path that invites you to
follow in the steps of those who have gone before.

The wisdom of the sages evolved, realized through the
experience of life in balance with the forces of nature.
The people traveled along the rivers, and through the
mountains, of the central plains of the Yellow River Valley.

As they rested by the fire at the days end, divinations were
cast, and stories were told. History was written on bones
and shells. Guided by the Divine, the closely held secrets
of the sages became the written language of the I Ching.

Seeking Your Destiny

To shape the future, your mind inspires your intention,
your wisdom motivates your actions. As you embark on
your journey you may not know where you are going.
Are you in search of your destiny?

The I Ching is a map of the balance of the universe.
It guides you to your destiny through self-awareness.
Travel now along the path of self-awareness.

The Balance of Harmony is Within the Self

The present moment nurtures the seeds of the future. The
power of your potential is just beyond the horizon. Are you
ready to seek the gift of good fortune? The journey begins
with your intention, as you seek the mysteries of the Tao.

Stories from the I Ching Book of Changes

Tossing the Coins

Select 3 coins of equal value.
Identify which side will equal 2,
and which side will equal 3.

Perform six-coin tosses to create a hexagram.
Jot down the number that totals each coin toss.
If the coin toss adds up to 6 or 8, draw a broken line.
If the coin toss adds up to 7 or 9, draw a solid line.

The first 3 lines are the lower trigram, side list.
The first toss is line 1, start from the bottom.
The second 3 lines are the upper trigram, top list.
The 6th coin toss is at the top.

First, find the lower trigram image in the left column.
Next find the image for the upper trigram in the top row.
Your number is the conjunction of the two trigrams.

The Changing Lines
When your coin toss results in a 6 or a 9 you will draw a new set of trigrams which will reveal the changes as a new hexagram. This new hexagram adds to your story, revealing the dynamic forces of change moving forward. As the lines change the energy moves up.

Casting With One Coin
For a quick and easy coin toss, use 1 coin. Determine which side is Yin, the other side will be Yang. The Yin side is a broken line, the Yang side is a solid line. Toss the coin 6 times, draw the lines, refer to the chart on the next page.

The Taoist Principle of Yin and Yang

Trigrams, 3 lines – Hexagrams, 6 Lines
The broken line is Yin, the solid line is Yang

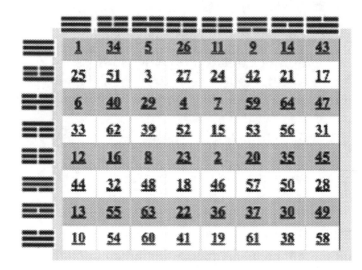

	1	34	5	26	11	9	14	43
	25	51	3	27	24	42	21	17
	6	40	29	4	7	59	64	47
	33	62	39	52	15	53	56	31
	12	16	8	23	2	20	35	45
	44	32	48	18	46	57	50	28
	13	55	63	22	36	37	30	49
	10	54	60	41	19	61	38	58

The Hexagram Chart

The hexagram chart is the map for which story you have chosen as the answer to your question. Please refer to the previous page for instructions on how to toss the coins.

The result of the coin toss will identify the hexagram number for the story that will guide you to the wisdom of the sages.

There is no easy way to capture the depth of the random number generator that is embodied in the I Ching as there are many authentic translations.

This book is not a translation, it is a journal of a life, lived long, with a copy of the I Ching tucked into my backpack.

The 8 Forces of Nature

That Which Always Is
The 8 Elements of change in the I Ching Book of Changes

Heaven, the dynamic force of yang.
The sun always rises and travels across the heavens.

Earth, the sustaining power of yin,
always supports and nurtures new life.

Fire creates and destroys,
always clinging to a source of fuel.

Water nourishes and replenishes,
always returning to the heart of the earth.

Thunder shocks and startles,
always awakening that which is sleeping.

The Mountain always stands firm in stillness,
its stability protects valuable resources.

The Wind always stimulates change,
gentle winds support, strong winds destroy.

The Lake and the joy of babbling brooks,
always travels along the path of least resistance.

To live in peace, one must be at peace.

That which is without,
shall not harm,
that which is within.

1 Sage Rides Six Dragons to Heaven

Good Fortune to Those Who Persevere

The legend of six dragons, the six stages of growth.

The primal power of the dynamic force
of yang energy represents the strength of heaven.

Seeking the power of the forces of creation,
the holy sage rides on the backs of six dragons,
to attain the power that establishes
a proper place, for all the lands and all the people.

The six lines of the hexagram represent the relationship
of Yin and Yang as they advance and decline.

Life emerges into the light,
as constant change inspires awareness
of the inevitable momentum,
of a beginning and an end for all things.

In the beginning of life on earth
the individual species evolved,
each with its own harmony with nature,
in conditions that ensured its survival.

Through perseverance the power
of the creative force expresses unlimited possibilities.

The virtues of the sage ensure the harmony of life.
Strength comes from within.

The Sublime is forever.
An unchanged and unchangeable force of creation.

Heaven Above - Heaven Below

Yang Energy Motivates the Dynamic Force of Creation

1 HEAVEN

Supported by the rotation of the seasons the ways of nature are absolute. The creative forces of the universe organize the perpetual motion of change.

The celestial powers of Heaven.
There are no conditions that can restrain
the forward march of time.

As you contemplate your well-being,
through the ceaseless action of time,
be aware that positive change, h

That which grows will wither,
that which withers will grow again,
this is the passage of time.

HEAVEN
*Cause and effect influence change to all things.
When I am in harmony with that which is absolute,
many great things can be achieved.
Only those who adhere to the enlightened path,
shall be empowered to influence my will.*

2 The Receptive Earth

Good fortune to those who recognize
when to act and when to wait

All living things dwell between heaven and earth.

The yin force of the earth supports creation
to achieve the eternal power of transformation.

It is the receptive nature of the earth
that ensures the manifestation of life.

The I Ching defines earth energy as the female horse.
The mare represents the responsive nature of the earth.

Through perseverance and devotion,
she transforms the potential of creativity into reality.

She roams the expanse of the land
with strength and swiftness, yet she is gentle.

Submitting to her role to nurture new life,
her actions conform to the natural laws of the universe.

In nature the times of spring and summer
support growth and change.

Fall and winter support harvest and storage.

Those who follow, by allowing themselves to be guided,
will learn from the situation.

For humanity the willingness to conform
to the demands of the situation invites success.

Earth Above - Earth Below

Magnetic Yin Energy, the Nurturing Force of the Earth

Through stillness,
the earth embraces all living things.
The primal power of Yin
responds to the primal power of Yang.

There are times to lead and times to follow.
It is wise to prepare for times of darkness and hardship.

In life be aware of the first signs of decay,
in this way the damage is minimized.

It is the sustaining power of perseverance
and good character that takes heed.

When there is no opportunity to advance,
It is best to submit to the times.

When there is work to be done join with those of like mind
to achieve that which you are willing to commit to.

EARTH
By holding fast to what is right
I gain the power of endurance.
Persevering, I remain firm in my commitments.
Until the time is right, I stand still,
waiting for the opportunity
to move forward from a stronger position.

3 Enduring the Struggle to Emerge

Good fortune as Misunderstandings are Resolved

All living things dwell between heaven and earth.

The beginning moves from nothing.

Perseverance creates order out of chaos.
Through perseverance the struggle
to survive takes form and life begins.

At the beginning there is danger,
both dark and light must exist in balance.
In difficult times, do not hasten to influence.

Engage in new beginnings only when the time is right.

That which is firm, and that which yields,
must be joined together. To lose your way
through arrogance invites misfortune.

A difficult path requires perseverance.
To gain the confidence of others, it is wise to be cautious.

Be faithful in your work.

The struggle to succeed requires
small efforts to overcome the existing danger.

Those with a clear vision can create order out of chaos.
Success to those who commit to right timing.

Water Above - Thunder Below

*The Chaos of Thunder Disperses the
Accumulation of Water*

3 Emerging

*Thunder and rain awaken that which
is emerging from beneath the soil.
As the storm passes the seeds of life
push up toward the light.*

The chaos of thunder unites with the power
of water and life emerges to fill the space.

Movement in dangerous times can be difficult.
Seek help to restore clarity of purpose.

Plan with confidence, in this way you may attract
those who can assist to avoid humiliation.

EMERGING
*The seeds were planted to grow new crops.
As time passes, we wait,
seeing nothing emerging from below.
Impatiently, to help the seeds emerge,
we remove some of the dirt.
Hastily we work to make it easier
for the seedlings to reach the light.
Exposed before their time,
the seedlings we helped withered and died.
Those that remained untouched emerged as a healthy crop.*

4 The Influence of a Wise Teacher

Seeking Good Fortune, the Folly of Youth Submits

The influence of what is already established guides the way.

Those without guidance in the ways of the world,
are inclined to be careless.

It is not through stupidity that the inexperienced
risk the mysteries of the unknown.

With no path to follow they proceed
without knowing where to go.

The feudal lords accumulate lands,
and organize the cultivation of agriculture.

The nomads are invited to join the community
to ensure safe expansion of the borders.

They are educated to conform to the demands
of society according to their abilities.

With strict discipline, and the student's
inner strength, awareness is mastered.

The teacher is patient.
Through perseverance the subject is covered thoroughly.

Like the folly of water, the inexperienced are innocent,
unaware of opportunities along the path of life.

*The innocence of youth
extends into all things newly discovered.*

Mountain Above - Water Below

The Innocence of Water

4 INNOCENCE

The steady flow
of falling rain is innocent,
unaware of where it goes.
The mountain is firm in its place,
the rain does not influence its stillness.

When water overflows its boundaries,
seeking its own way,
there is the chaos of uncertainty.

Trapped within the heart of the mountain,
the water conforms to the demands of its environment.

This is the time to follow the path long established.

The inexhaustible wisdom of the universe,
will enrich all things.

The wisdom of the ages
enlightens those who seek simplicity.

INNOCENCE
Many times, I don't know what to do.
Wishing to take the path of least resistance,
I seek those who are willing to show me the way.
To influence the path of an enlightened future,
I invite those who are willing to learn from my experience.

5 Waiting for the Rain

Good Fortune Often Results
From Ways That are Strange to us

The destiny of the people depends on nourishment.

Life on earth depends on the falling of the rain.

Without rain, the future is uncertain.

If there is too much rain, knowing
the potential for the inevitable, we wait.

We bide our time with inner strength.

Aware that we cannot interfere with destiny,
we fortify ourselves with nourishment and gladness.

In this way, by continuing in our daily life,
we guard against wasting our strength.

As the storm approaches
we know that danger may defeat us.

Seeking its traditional path, the water flows
to the depths beneath the mountain;
only to return to heaven
forming clouds to nourish the future.

When the river is rising one must cross the stream
with enough strength to persevere.

Water Above - Heaven Below

Heaven Supports the Clouds
The Clouds Collect the Rain

Clouds are forming,
yet we must wait for the rain
to nourish all things.
Like waiting for the rain to fall,
we wait for destiny
to determine our fate.

Joyously we watch the clouds form in the sky,
knowing that change in approaching.

When there is no time for error, we persevere in our tasks.
When seeking help from others we show respect.

Through inner strength
we do not fall into the mud of uncertainty.

Our strength is not compromised by the fear of danger.

WAITING
There is an uneasy feeling in the wind.
I am aware that things are changing.
Through this awareness I wait.
When change is imminent unrest arises.
Fortifying myself in the face of danger,
I remain calm, knowing that I have
the strength to act when needed.

6 Dilemma of the Arrogant Dragon

Those Who Submit to Creation
Walk the Path of Good Fortune

The I Ching refers to the "Arrogant Dragon"
as that which enforces through force.

The dragon symbolizes the energy of heaven,
moving upward toward the light.

All things are in their correct place,
yet there is conflict within the community.

There is danger when those in a weak position
feel trapped by those in power.

To escape their circumstances,
they may cause conflict through cunning and guile.

Through willfulness, and fixed determination,
they obstruct progress by seeking the easy way.

Clarity from the beginning will avoid confusion.

To seek resolution through arbitration, leaders find
an authority who can mediate an impartial decision.

The way to a fair conclusion, when dealing with
a difficult situation is to assume the middle way.

To continue without resolution is harmful to all.
Those who win by force will lose by force.

There is no distinction to winning
simply by being stronger than your adversary.

Heaven Above Water Below

The Ascending Force of Heaven
The Descending Force of Water

True to their nature
heaven and water each move
in their own direction.
Those in high positions must
be aware of the power of those below.

The cosmic force of water flows downward,
only to be trapped in the depths of the abyss.

Having no power to escape it waits.
There is danger as it accumulates enough power to emerge.

When you are being obstructed, even though you
are correct, avoid taking the conflict too far.

By yielding the issue may be resolved.
If the conflict persists, take immediate action.

Whenever possible do not perpetuate, turn away.

DILEMMA
When I am being obstructed, I look within.
How could I have avoided
the confusion which led to the conflict?
First, I must seek advice from those who know me well.
Whether I am right or wrong,
I consider what I am willing to do to gain
the peace of mind that comes with resolution.

7 The Discipline of a Peaceful Majority

Good fortune to Those Who Dwell
Within the Shelter of the Peaceful Majority

Water accumulates and is stored
within the caverns of the earth.

Even though the water is invisible the people are at peace,
knowing that the source is ready for their use when needed.

Through accumulation of resources, like the storage of
water, the people gathered to establish safe boundaries.

A legion of people massed together to respond to conflicts.

Military training enabled the cooperation of the peasants.

Discipline leads them out of danger through cooperation.

The legion is called upon only when a valid cause exists.

The enthusiasm of a strong leader
captures the hearts of the people.

The legions became and army which restored order.

As time passes a proper and humane government
is established to enact the will of the people.

The goal of great leaders is to shelter the people,
and prosper through right action.

Earth Above - Water Below

The Earth Shelters the Accumulation of Water

*The community assembles in a place
where resources are readily available.
Through unity and generosity,
a just cause provides
the will to succeed.*

Just as the power of the water
is accumulated within the earth.
the power of the people accumulates
to establish the strength of secure borders.

It is your experience, and good judgment,
that enables you to acquire the support
of those who can speak for the majority.

Discipline requires the willpower to advance your goals.

Be clear in your intention.

DISCIPLINE
*Without discipline I cannot lead,
nor can I follow.
I am one of many who accumulate resources.
Seeking order, I am cautious in my relationships.
In times of danger,
I remain loyal to my companions.
I cannot stand alone.*

8 The Rivers of Your Destiny

*Good Fortune as Self-Interest Submits
to Awareness of the Needs of the Community*

Ancient kings unite with the princes,
and the people, to establish a common goal.

People organize themselves by conforming
to the needs of the community.

Those who follow must agree, of their own free will.
Each must comply without hesitation.

Like water, which fills all empty spaces,
and holds together, human society prospers
through the mutual efforts of the community.

Those who lead unify the people with confidence
in the conformity of a common purpose.

Leaders must be sincere and able
to avoid confusion through organization.
Through perseverance, and unity,
they work together for the well-being of all.

Stragglers, those who hesitate may regret, as they
may not be welcome to join later.

Just as water flows to join with that which has gone before,
the unity of relationship is established through solidarity,
with the common culture of historical heritage.

***It is fundamental that truth, loyalty,
and sincerity are the foundations of relationship.***

Water Above - Earth Below

Water Supported by Earth, the Unity of Relationship

8 UNITY

Yielding to the laws of nature,
water follows its traditional path.
Joining in the lakes and rivers,
it returns to the caverns
within the heart of the earth.

Seek the relationship of mutual support,
and join with those of like mind.

Do not throw yourself away by standing alone,
or joining with the wrong people.

Those who follow the path of tradition,
have the power to attract support.

Look within yourself and inquire again,
are you able to embrace serenity and constancy?

Will you gather the strength to commit to the sublime?

UNITY
I am a stream in the river of my ancestors' dreams.
I inherit their progress for the conditions of humanity.
It is through the wisdom
of their traditions that I am strong.
I celebrate their rituals established over centuries.
Now, I am the ancestor,
I seek to fulfill my responsibilities
to the generations of those who I will never know.

9 Gentle Winds Scatter the Clouds

Gentleness Influences Good Fortune Through Restraint

The wind drives across heaven,
clouds accumulate, eventually there will be rain.

China, 11th century BCE, King Wen visited
the court of the tyrannical ruler King Zhou of Shang.

The tyrant of Shang, fearing King Wen's growing power,
imprisoned him for seven years.

At that time the I Ching consisted only of the 64 hexagrams.

Many gifts were offered
to influence the release of King Wen.

During his time in prison King Wen translated
the archetypes of the hexagrams to create
the original text for the current version of the I Ching.

Through gentle persuasion,
and the gift of valuable lands, he was released.

Returning to his home he secretly
plotted to muster enough strength to defeat the tyrant.

King Wen set the example for the image of accumulating
strength to achieve a goal.

His power of restraint
avoided creating a situation in which he could not prevail.

*A weak position restrains the fulfillment of a desirable
outcome as those in power present an obstacle.*

Wind Above - Heaven Below

The Power of Persuasion Weathers the Storm

9 RESTRAINT

*Only a strong wind can collect
enough moisture to bless the land.
The gentle winds restrain the accumulation
of clouds,
yet there is no rain.*

Strength grows as time passes,
true to course the rain will fall.

Water nourishes all things, crops are planted,
and stored to sustain through difficult times.

When you encounter obstructions,
it is best to exert influence in small ways.

To force change now is not in harmony with the times.

Return to the way that is best suited for the situation.

To influence the process of change,
be restrained and proceed with caution.

RESTRAINT
*Hand in hand and arm to arm,
we influence the ways of the world.
Gently, remembering my commitment to myself,
I do not suffer misfortune by reacting to extremes.
Working in small ways I refine my character.
Tolerating the times,
I share my wealth with my neighbors.*

10 The Tail of the Tiger

Those who are Content to do Good Work
Invite Good Fortune, Success Follows

The mythical tiger held the balance
of the cosmic forces within the Universe.

Five tigers, representing the five seasons of change,
are responsible for the balance of power,
and the intangible forces of nature.

The supreme force of the unseen,
the tiger represents success and achievement.

With cautious effort, taking care does not entice danger,
those with no power approach the king.

The ruler remains correct, honoring the "Will of Heaven".

The tiger represents risk, and uncertainty.
To become arrogant there is danger.

Throughout the ages, and all cultures,
the social rank remains the primary structure of society.

Those without influence persuade
with laughter and good cheer.

With composure and respect
the weak influence the strong in small ways.

Heaven Above - Lake Below

Heaven Above the Lake, Each in its Correct Place

10 TREADING

It is good to take a stand
toward those with power.
With respect and good humor,
the weak tread
upon the tail of the tiger.

The dynamic harmony of yin and yang
supports the balance of constant change.

In difficult situations, only hidden power
can influence in small ways.

With gentle persuasion they tread lightly,
their power is within.

It is through good conduct
that one may move forward without blame.

To rule from an honored place
be mindful of those who challenge.

TREADING
To assume the role of leadership,
I inherit the vulnerability of those who must follow.
Not all will conduct themselves in the correct way.
I seek the support of those who are cheerful,
and content within themselves.
In this way my efforts are not wasted on those,
whose goals do not support what I intend to achieve.

11 The Turning Point

Balance Sets the Roots of Good Fortune
Unity Sets the Potential for Balance Within the Self

The grass grows between heaven and earth.
From the roots grow the blades,
intertwined by the roots beneath the soil.

A single blade of grass cannot exist alone,
it is one blade amongst many. To uproot the grass,
the soil which it clings to must also be removed.

The king in the north gives his daughter
in holy marriage to the king in the south.

The union of opposites with equal power to influence,
supports the balance of harmony.

The people see the wilderness across the river
where the ways of the uncultured prevail.

Seeking harmony with those beyond,
the strongest of the worthy reach out.

Fording the river, they approach
the remote regions of the kingdom with gentleness.

A gradual increase in communication
sets the roots of unity for the entire region.

The special interests of the powerful are avoided.

The people work together to sustain harmony and success.

Undesirable factions are held in check
but cannot be permanently abolished.

Earth Above - Heaven Below

The Balance of Heaven on Earth

11 BALANCE

The influence of darkness departs
as the power of the creative approaches.
The balance of growth and decline
work together toward a common goal.

This is a time of unobstructed positive energy,
what is above is united with what is below.

Families unite for mutual benefit
as the strong support the weak.

At the tipping point the days grow longer,
only to grow shorter once more.

Organize your life with awareness of the ways of nature.

Choose the middle way to transform
your internal struggle of advance and decline.

BALANCE
I see through the illusion of prosperity,
to maintain my commitment to the middle way.
In times of decline, I am reminded
that balance is the harmony within.
When I am at peace, good fortune will not desert me.

12 The Stagnation of Obstruction

Waiting for Spring in Stillness Until Good Fortune Returns

Forward motion has reached its peak
and begins to sink into decline.

Autumn represents a time when expansion withdraws.
It is the season of harvest and storage of that which sustains.

There is peace, a time of standing still,
preparing for the stagnation of winter.

The dropping of fruit from the trees,
and seeds from the flowers, notifies the village.

The birds do not fly, knowing that it is time
to prepare their nests to protect through dark times.

Hinderance imposes hardship on the people.

Weak leadership, and obstruction of justice,
influence the stagnation of progress.

The strong withdraw, avoiding inclusion,
quietly awaiting the opportunity to return.

As the creative force ascends, difficulties withdraw.

Positive energy and order are restored.
The people plant their seeds and celebrate.

Heaven Above - Earth Below

Heaven and Earth go Their Separate Ways

*That which can be accomplished
has reached its zenith.
Standing still we contemplate
the forces of advance and decline.*

12 STAGNATION

The earth remains still as it prepares for spring.

True to its purpose, it quietly nurtures new growth.

Within each person there are times of decline.
The wise contemplate their inner worth.

Those who hold fast to their principles
remain faithful through stillness.

In good time the opportunity for expansion ascends
as the influence of decline withdraws in the spring.

STAGNATION
*Regardless of the season, this is a time of struggle.
It is wise to know when to stand still.
The light grows weak as the dark ascends.
Hence the nature of constant change
impacts the lives of the people.
Advance and decline continue through eternity.
This is the way of the world.*

13 The Door is Open

Good Fortune to Those who Commit to an Open Mind

The door is open to King Wen's goal
for an alliance among the people of the region.

The clans gathered to establish common goals.

To encourage harmony, the countrymen
re organized according to their common interests.

With the alliance of clarity within, and strength without,
the leaders organized the forces according to lineage.

A plan was authorized to protect the region at the borders.

With the strength of many,
the troops gathered in the hills,
and sheltered amongst the trees.

Gaining strength when the time was right
King Wu, the son of King Wen, launched a successful
assault against the unruly nomadic tribes to the north.

The universal concerns of humanity
established an alliance among the many.

Open discussion is established among people who are equal.
Those with low motives are discouraged.

The tyrant of Shang is forced to yield.
The alliance of the common people is united in harmony.

*Leadership earned through good character
rather than authority brings lasting order.*

Heaven Above - Fire Below

Fire Reaches up to Heaven Seeking Harmony

The source of power rises.
Strength through the universal
force of creation.
The luminaries of heaven
establish awareness
of the passing of time.

Heaven above represents union.
The sun shines upon all things equally.

Fire below represents
the organization of forward movement,
which reaches up to heaven.

It is not your private interests that nurture
the organization of a successful community.

The union of strength within allows your ego
to step beyond the gate of self-interest.

UNION
It is through my willingness,
to appreciate the opinions of others,
that I am willing to grow and change.
I do not force my divergent views upon my neighbors.
When I am willing to yield to the majority,
the door will open to harmony within.

14 It Takes a Big Wagon

With Strength and Ingenuity
There is the Promise of Good Fortune

It is the time of great wealth and an abundant harvest.

The people share in the prosperity
of an organized community.

Circumstances are favorable
for authorities to unite the people.

Leadership is with those who are modest and kind.

Able bodied workers join
to achieve success without hinder or blame.

The king is humble,
knowing the secret of harmony is with the people.

Surrounded by strong and willing helpers
that stand at his side, he is dignified.

When difficulties arose, they remained informed
of opportunities to avoid mistakes.

In this way, they worked together
with clarity, fairness, and an unselfish attitude.

It takes a big wagon to carry the heavy load
organization serves by establishing order.

Fire Above - Heaven Below

The Abundance of Heaven on Earth

Strength and clarity unite,
the sun is shining on all things.
Success is achieved with the support
of loyal and trusted friends.

14 ABUNDANCE

When undertaking a project, that requires
the help of others, be generous with your possessions.

Avoid blame by remaining free of arrogance.

Be liberal in your attitude
toward exclusive use of personal property.

Share your wealth with your neighbors
and it will be returned to you in many ways.

ABUNDANCE
As the flow of time moves forward into
a favorable position for success.
Actions are arranged
to bring well-being to all.
In abundance I seek to support those
who lead, through benevolence.
In scarcity I join with others,
to lighten the load of recovery.

15 To Cultivate Modesty Begin with the Heart

To Cross the Great River with Respect
Assures the Good Fortune of Self-Discipline

The re-distribution of power into regions
established the beginning of feudalism in China.

Unification was achieved by linking
the individual clans into one focused legion.

Preparations were made to challenge
the barbarian rulers of Shang in the northwest.

At the heart of the action was the humbleness is the king,
whose desire was for all people to live in peace.

The sources of social discontent,
caused by inequality, are made equal.

To establish order, and equalize extremes,
requires working together toward a common goal.

Through the redistribution of excess,
what is empty is made full, and what is full is made empty.

High mountains are worn down and valleys are filled up.
That which is high yields to that which is low.

Those who approach with awareness are humble,
acting only when the time is right.

Wise behavior and an unassuming attitude
can accomplish even difficult tasks.

Earth Above - Mountain Below

Stillness at the Heart of the Mountain
There is Peace

Through modesty success
is achieved through
the balance of equality.
Great strength is balanced
by the virtue of humility.

The light, of that which is great,
shines upon all things equally.

It is the way of nature to balance all things
as dynamic and magnetic energies attract each other.

The fullness of the sun at midday yields to the darkness.
Emptiness, as total darkness yields to the dawn.

As decline withdraws strength returns,
with the promise of the light.

Through modesty, what is difficult is made easy,
for those who understand the ways of the world.

MODESTY
When my heart is full, I have resources to share.
Effortlessly I exert a lasting influence on others.
Through modesty I earn the support
needed to accomplish my goals.
Through discipline I create structure within myself,
as I approach those I seek to influence.

16 The Joys and Mysteries of Life

Good Fortune, Together the Harvest Will Sustain Us

"The Mandate of Heaven"
The king establishes his privilege to rule above all others.

The tyrant of Shang to the north
is declared to have lost the "Mandate of Heaven".

The king sets armies to march and lords to rule.

The uniting of the clans was established
to secure safe borders.

Organization to protect the boundaries
resulted in a hierarchy of nobility and commoners.

Harmony prevails as the officials
mobilize the army with order and discipline.

The holy, are forgiven,
and the fines and punishments are fair.

Through joy they contemplate the future,
with the understanding that events,
will occur in the natural order with fixed regularity.

*Friends and families gather to rejoice
in honor of the wisdom of the ancestors.*

Thunder Above - Earth Below

The Harmony of Movement
Thunder Rolls Across the Earth

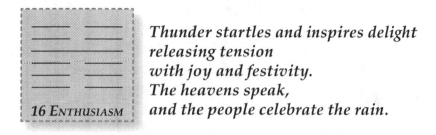

Thunder startles and inspires delight
releasing tension
with joy and festivity.
The heavens speak,
and the people celebrate the rain.

16 ENTHUSIASM

Just as thunder releases tension in the heavens,
and rain showers down upon the earth.

Celebrations with music and dance,
release tensions through joy and enthusiasm.

Be humble in your tasks.

Focus on what you wish to achieve,
with awareness of the mysterious ways of nature.

ENTHUSIASM
I stay in tune with the natural laws
of stillness and movement.
Following those who recognize
the needs of my community
I am reawakened
to the joys and mysteries of life.
Through co-operation and enthusiasm
I speak only when the time is right.

17 Those Who Lead Must Also Follow

*Good Fortune as Movement and Rest
are in Balance with the Times*

The domestication of the ox and horse
supported transport through difficult terrain.

The joy of movement during long and tedious journeys
required enthusiasm from all who traveled.

Leaders adapted to the limitations of their followers.

Care Is taken to provide the necessary periods of rest,
and recuperation, to support the effort.

Through adaptation the effort of the long sojourn
gives way to rest at the end of the day.

As the days grow darker the lords gathered
the clans to celebrate and rejoice.

The tireless activities of the summer
give way to rest and recuperation at night.

The faithful are rewarded
as the sage reveals the path to the ways of heaven.

The king travels to the western mountains in reverence,
seeking the wisdom of the ancestors.

*Strong leaders support followers
with joyous activities, cooperation, and right action.*

Lake Above - Thunder Below

Thunder Rests Beneath the Lake

17 FOLLOWING

The dynamic force of electricity
lingers within the lake.
As the seasons change the forces
of nature promise the inevitable.

As winter approaches thunder and lightening
withdraw to rest until clouds form above the lake.
The people adapt to the changing of the season.

This is a time to commit yourself to releasing
the stress of constant progress.

The willingness to join with others
is needed to achieve your goals.

Reflect on your situation,
seek harmony with those who can assist.

Only when these conditions are met,
can you ask, others to follow.

FOLLOWING
Rest in knowing that great things are achieved,
through the cooperation of a like-minded society.
By following the laws of adaptation,
I can realize my intentions.
Supreme success through perseverance
and commitment to right action.

18 The Mistakes of the Past

Moving Forward Without Fear Supports Good Fortune

The wind blows low on the mountain,
there is danger of decay in the fields.

When decay and stagnation persist,
there is work to be done.

In the lives of the people indifference
combined with inertia causes corruption.

Decay through rigid adherence to tradition
must be addressed in an orderly fashion.

The next generation is held responsible
to consciously generate change when needed.

When there is opportunity
for reform of attitudes from the past,
that which is no longer working is acknowledged.

Consideration must be taken
for what caused the decay before action is taken.

Through appropriate change
the generations of the future will achieve reformation.

A new beginning will require awareness
of the corrections needed to avoid relapse.

Mountain Above - Wind Below

Stagnation and Abuse
are Passed Down Through Generations

18 THE PAST

The abuse of human freedom.
The image of stagnation.
Work on what has been spoiled.
Strict adherence to tradition
leads to danger.

When change is upon you, it is wise to wait
three days before planning a new course.

If no action is taken, to make a correction,
a new beginning must be considered.

This is your gift to future generations.

THE PAST
Awareness of my attachment to the past,
rectifies what has been spoiled in my life.
I give thanks to my father,
seeing where there is work to be done.
I am grateful to my mother,
aware that this is the time to set things right.
By setting right what has been spoiled,
my strength of spirit will remedy
the mistakes of the past.

19 The Awakening of Spring

The Inexhaustible Source of Great Leadership
Brings Good Fortune to the People

Spring approaches, the days grow longer,
the earth awakens, warmed by the sun.

The time has come for new growth and expansion.

The light of spring ascends to take its place in expansion,
the wise create a bond that unites in a common goal.

There is awareness that the increasing light
will surely turn again toward darkness.

Joy, and the prospect of abundance,
prevails as the return-to-work approaches.

The sage returns from the mountain,
overseeing the progress with tolerance for the people.

Consequences may set in for those who fail
to understand the importance of timing.

Shock and remorse can be avoided
by engaging those who are strong and efficient.

When those who lead are inexhaustible in their
commitment to govern with tolerance and perseverance,
those who follow are protected.

Fate may bring misfortune, to those
who do not move forward when the time is right.

Earth Above - Lake Below

The Lake Dwells Within the Caverns Beneath the Earth

19 AWAKENING

The earth, on which all life depends,
represents the many.
The collection and storage of water
provides sustenance to all living things.

The lakes have evaporated, forming clouds.
Clouds bring the rain which floods the rivers.

Be prepared for the approach of adversity
and all that it demands.

As time passes,and darkness approaches,
caution is essential.

With give and take, through contemplation of what is right,
you need not yield to fate.

With joy and respect proceed toward your goals,
with perseverance and good timing.

AWAKENING
That which has withdrawn into darkness
ascends toward the light of new beginnings.
It is the changing of the seasons.
Abundance returns as the approach of spring awakens.
Be sure footed, power comes from within.
This is the time to do what must be done.

20 The King Contemplates the People

*Good Fortune to Those who do not Sacrifice
Their Path to the Will of Others*

In ancient China the kingdom was ruled
from a place that towered above the village.

This lofty position implied
that those who rule are closer to heaven.

From the safety of this great height the king
was able to view far and wide.

What is seen below establishes
awareness of the ways of the people.

The government aligns the activities
of the community with the laws of nature.

Rules are established according to the seasons of the region.

In this way local customs were developed
to establish order that served through generations.

The laws are honored with ceremony,
the expression of trust in all that is sacred.

*Wisdom is achieved through experience
the answers have always been there.*

Wind Above - Earth Below

The Wind Travels Freely Over the Earth

*A view from above has the power
to influence all things.
The king observes
the needs of the people,
and follows the wisdom of the sage.*

Time has passed,
yet the wind still blows across the earth,
unhindered by expectations.

Before you decide to advance or retreat,
consider your own position.

Your experience is your gift to the future.

Do not peek through the crack in the door
like a child who is constrained by circumstance.

Your ability to manifest is an ongoing process.

CONTEMPLATION
*We have come to a place in society
where there are no rulers.
We are ruled by the majority,
those who speak up.
Observing the circumstances of my community,
I fear that those in power serve only themselves.
Contemplating my situation
I ask, am I able to speak up?*

21 The Power of the Storm

Persevere in Dark Times, Stay on Course
Good Fortune Awaits Beyond the Horizon

The balance of positive and negative energies.

The king has defeated the tyrant but the surviving
ruling class of the Shang Dynasty is creating disharmony.

Those who command are gentle and fair in their policies.

Commerce and articles of trade are available
at the marketplace and the village is full of activity.

Those who transgress the laws of the land
are deterred with just measure.

Vigorous action is taken to constrain
those who will not yield to the law.

Clearly defined penalties are established
to ensure unity and harmony.

The penalties are public, administered with the
clarity of lightening, and the shock of thunder.

Guilt and innocence are determined
through appropriate legal proceedings.

Punishment is firm and clear
with penalties that fit the consequences of the crime.

Throughout history penalties are decided
through the correct administration of the laws

Fire Above - Thunder Below

The Awakening of Awareness

21 THE STORM

The power of the storm
commands respect.
Nature inspires,
foretold is forewarned.
As the storm passes tension is released,
and obstacles are overcome.

The sun shines down upon the earth.

When disharmony obstructs your life,
and impedes your progress,
be clear in your goals.

Just as lightning and thunder instill respect
for the power of nature, your actions should be taken,
with respect for the boundaries of correct behavior.

That which obstructs must be dealt with,
even through force when there is no other way.

When facing a difficult situation,
or an obstinate opponent,
be firm and persevering.

THE STORM
If you expect to be treated with fairness,
be willing to sacrifice that which you covet,
for the comfort of remaining free of fear.
It is through understanding the ways of nature,
that you are safe in your understanding of yourself.

22 The Perfection of Grace

Good Fortune to Those who Give no Excess to Extremes

The king walks beside the carriage
as he mingles with the people of the village.

He is modest, knowing that
to assume external adornments will lead to danger.

When seeking perfection,
the king remains within the bounds of tradition.

Beyond the village the mountain is stable in its place.

Firm stillness within, unconcerned with beauty,
the mountain remains true to its nature.

Just as the world is beautiful,
and free of struggle for existence,
there is grace for those whose inner beauty
does not require opulence through external form.

Even though this is a time of balance,
it is not a good time to attempt to make major changes.

Through dark times the king remains still
until the return of more favorable circumstances.

Through the will to silence pride grace is achieved.

Mountain Above - Fire Below

The Harmony of Balance
Fire at the Boot of the Mountain

22 GRACE

The glow of the fire is far reaching,
the mountain remains still.
Beauty does not change
the firm stillness within the mountain.

The image of perfection with the grace of inner strength.

To contemplate the heavens, in this time of clarity,
remain firm to your adherence to simplicity.

With awareness of the passage of time
you can shape your world.

You are supported by the strength
of the people in your life.

GRACE
If I wish to live in a state of perfection,
I choose the ideal and reject simplicity.
It is through the contemplation,
of clarity within and strength without,
that I remain true
to the ideals of the dignity of Grace.

23 The Opportunity of Misfortune

Good Fortune, as Dark Becomes Light,
and Decrease Becomes Increase

The mountain, firm and strong with a broad base,
does not yield to instability.

The laws of nature prevail,
instability eventually destroys itself.

A mountain proud and steep,
with a narrow base is unstable
there is danger of collapse.

Even though the mountain
reaches upward toward the light,
it is dependent on the stability
of the dark earth below for support.

Likewise, when those who lead
have little concern for the people,
support is withdrawn.

With too much weight at the top
the stability of authority collapses.

New leadership is aware that success
requires the support of the people.
Devoted and calm, the new leadership
re-establishes a broad base of support.

Care is taken to empower the people
with generosity and kindness.

When circumstances decline and darkness encroaches,
wise leaders are benevolent.

Mountain Above - Earth Below

The Mountain rests upon the Earth

23 INSTABILITY

The stability of the mountain
relies on the stability of the earth.
If the earth moves
the mountain could fall.
What was high becomes low.

In times of chaos uncertainty
invites the opportunity for change.

When instability invites disruption,
the security of the future becomes precarious.

The forces of nature command
the balance of advance and decline.

Through dark times remain still,
until the return of more favorable circumstances.

You are supported by the strength
of the people in your life.

INSTABILITY
There is an opportunity now for a new beginning.
Turn away from chaos, the danger has passed.
Remain loyal and grounded in stillness.
Align with a like-minded community,
knowing that at the turning point,
the darkness will surely yield to the light.

24 A Glimmer of Light in the Darkness

The Promise of Spring
Good Fortune Inspires the Worthy

The fruit has fallen from the tree,
melting into the earth.

What was old relents and yields
to the approach of a new beginning.

The seeds of new beginnings
remain committed to new life.

The depths of darkness.
Thunder rumbles from the center of the earth.

The king closes the passes,
merchants and strangers do not move about.

Those who understand the custom of resting gain strength.

At the turning point,
the darkness reaches its extreme,
longer days bring promise.

As the darkness withdraws the creative force returns.
Daily tasks are restored, and recovery begins.

Eventually winter passes, and the days grow warmer.
The comings and goings of daily life returns to the village.

Regret withdraws as remorse is balanced
by the self-reflection of the cycles of change

Earth Above - Thunder Below

The Thunder of Spring Rests Within the Earth

24 RECOVERY

*Winter solstice, the people return
to their homes to rest.
At the turning point
the depth of darkness
relents to the promise of spring.*

The arousing energy of thunder remains hidden.

If you have lost your way, this is the turning point.
The darkness of winter cannot last forever.

Restore daily habits that support well-being,
make firm decisions to prepare yourself
for a new beginning.

When chaos and darkness shatter
your internal clarity, choose your destiny
to avoid the dangers of opposition.

Return to peace within,
it is good to have somewhere to go.

RECOVERY
*Regardless of circumstances there is constant change.
Darkness and danger are inevitable.
This is a time to know your relationship,
with the forces of the universe.
Move only when the time is right.
The light returns from rest, with awareness of the Divine.
Until then be goodhearted, remain calm, and rest.*

25 The Innocent Clarity of Intuition

Good Fortune as the Innocent Move Forward

The shock of thunder, the stability of summer,
yields to the forces of winter.

Wind and thunder roll across the plains,
arousing movement through the unexpected.

The unexpected awareness of danger,
signifies the time to act.

Life evolves without ulterior motives,
according to the demands of the times.

Bewilderment, and failure to prepare, leads to misfortune.

The innocence of the subconscious
guides our actions through the will of creation.

When misfortune imposes, there is no blame.
At the correct time, firmness of action ensures success.

When setbacks occur through no fault of your own,
remain true to yourself.

Seek the way to move forward
in harmony with the times without fear or blame.

When the shock of misfortune comes from within,
return to innocence before making decisions.

Heaven Above - Thunder Below

The Strength of Creation Shines Down Upon the Earth

25 INTUITION

Consciousness is awakened
by the unexpected.
The innocence of nature
drives the actions of change,
and transformation.

Even though the thunder startles,
that which is without
shall not harm that which is within.

The wisdom of nature, free of insincerity,
dwells within the heart.

Intuition guides the way,
to inspire the will to achieve your goals.

Devote your attention to what you need to do today.

Moving forward undertake each action with a calm mind.

With new awareness,
seek the origin of unintentional misfortune.

INTUITION
It is my intuition that guides my actions.
I know that nature's order and right timing
will nurture and support my growth.
Through meditation I remain connected
to the universal laws of creation.

26 The Nurturance of Prosperity

The Path of Good Fortune is Open to all
Leaders Will Lead and Followers Will Follow

We see the clouds forming
in the valleys between the peaks.

Reaching up, above the clouds, the mountain stands firm.

There will be rain, we wait,
knowing that as time passes, we must be prepared.

The force of great power is tamed
through the daily practice of self-discipline.

Keeping still, until circumstances
are favorable, we nourish our virtues.

With commitment to the innocent
the people are cared for and nourished.

When danger has been forestalled,
success is possible through right action and right timing.

There is the potential for great undertakings.

Through restraint new energy accumulates
for the cultivation of potentials.

The creative is supported by stillness.

Moving forward, with courage, we cross the great river.

Hidden treasures of the past
hold firm to the wisdom of the ancestors.

Mountain Above - Heaven Below

Heaven Supports the Mountain
with a Constant Flow of Positive Energy

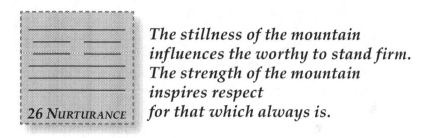

26 NURTURANCE

The stillness of the mountain
influences the worthy to stand firm.
The strength of the mountain
inspires respect
for that which always is.

Strength of character is supported
by the perpetual energy of the source.

When facing interference
the unworthy should not be confronted directly.

Bide your time until difficulties can be dealt with
by eradicating the source at the root.

When the way has cleared, move forward,
with the help of those who are of like mind.

NURTURANCE
During quiet times,
daily routines accumulate resources.
When you approach a great challenge,
study those who have succeeded in the past.
During times of danger the wise remain composed.
With strong commitment to the task,
wait until the time is right, and friends are near.

27 The Self Reliance of the Magic Tortoise

To Seek Good Fortune be Temperate
in What you Desire for Yourself

Honor the ways of the *"Magic Tortoise"*
as a symbol of divine guidance and self-reliance.

Independent, this mythical creature lives only on air,
with no need of earthly nourishment.

In ancient times the tortoise was a symbol of independence.

It possesses the dignity of the sage in its ability
to be self-reliant, and able to adapt
to the conditions of the times.

Good fortune to those who, in pursuit of independence,
seek the ways of the sage.

Actions taken from a position of tranquility,
are able, to nourish what is right.

Those who pursue self-satisfaction and pleasure
will wander from the path losing their way.

Those, who are able, to create
renewable resources are supported in their endeavors.

The wisdom to nourish others,
establishes the ability to nourish the self.

Through self-reliance there are provisions
for the needs of all things that dwell upon the earth.

Actions taken from a position of tranquility
are willing to nourish what is right.

Mountain Above - Thunder Below

*The Stillness of the Mountain
is Awakened by the Thunder of Spring*

27 NOURISH

*When the time is right,
stillness is transformed into movement.
Those of good character cultivate
the nourishment of self-reliance.*

The legend of the "Magic Tortoise" inspires awareness
of the importance of being in control of your own destiny.

First one must consider what is planted,
and when it will be harvested.

Work must be done to establish long term benefits.

When the freedom of self-reliance is lost,
like the tortoise when captured, there will be misfortune.

The cultivation of character benefits
when movement is preceded by stillness.

Those who are independent
place great value on their freedom.

Through strength of spirit, you need not seek support.

NOURISH
*Through knowing when to rest and when to act.
When to speak and when to remain silent.
I am able, to nourish myself through good work,
and nourish others with contemplation and tranquility.*

28 The Breaking Point

Good Fortune to Those who Seek Support
Along the Path of a New Beginning

The water has risen above the trees,
the situation is unstable.

The old tree stands firm,
sending down stronger roots to support stability.

Even though there is the intention
for new growth the tree remains still.

Withdrawing from the goals of the future,
it stands alone without regret.

When the task is too great, there is no blame
for the actions required to avoid misfortune.

As the danger withdraws,
there is a time of new beginnings.

The old willow tree sprouts new shoots.

In the village, like new growth from an old tree,
an old man takes a young wife to secure his future.

In this way the danger of exhaustion
is transformed into the potential for new growth.

Harmony returns as hardships are transformed.

When the wisdom within is greater than the danger
Without those with inner strength remain steadfast.

Water Above - Wood Below

The Crisis of Excess, Hardship in Extraordinary Times

In times of great excess
caution is required
as progress is not supported.
In extraordinary times,
the wise withdraw undaunted by fear.

This is a time when the weight
of excess force has reached the breaking point.

There may be forces that pose unmovable obstructions.

Reduce the potential for collapse by stepping back.

It is better to stand alone than to move forward into danger.

Take care to make choices to secure a strong position.

Be open allowing new and fresh ideas,
do not seek to stand firm in rigidity.

In this way mistakes can be avoided.

EXCESS
Take heed of the times.
Caution is not fear, it is wisdom.
In setting goals be aware.
When the forces against you are strong,
it is good to have somewhere to go.
Seek the support of those without ulterior motives.

29 Danger on The Path of Least Resistance

Good Fortune to Those who Remain
Aware of the Heart of the Situation

The rain falls upon the earth.

When the lake is full, the rivers flow.

There is danger as the water overflows its banks.

Water seeks the path of least resistance
as it returns to the place of its ancestors,
at the center of the earth, beneath the mountain.

If the path is narrow and steep,
unaware of the dangers, there is no escape.

The laws of the universe force it to plunge downward,
no matter how steep the descent.

With no way out, the river follows the narrow path.

Eventually it reaches its goal, no matter the obstacles.

Innocent of the chaos it has caused along the way,
it is trapped within the abyss beneath the mountain.

To understand the path to success,
consult with those who have endured,
the dangers of the past.

Do not grow accustomed to danger,
as repetition of danger is foolhardy.

Water Above - Water Below

Water Always Flows to the Heart of the Earth

29 DANGER

*When clouds accumulate
the rain must fall.
Innocent of its true nature,
water flows along
the rivers of its ancestors.*

The human heart dwells safely
within the boundaries of the body.

When you are confronted with a dangerous situation,
be cautious of the path of least resistance.

At this time, only that which must be done
to avoid disaster should be of concern.

In this way actions that are taken
will lead to the desired outcome.

DANGER
*With respect for the power
of the forces of nature,
I am consistent in my awareness.
When surrounded by danger,
I do not lose my way.
Waiting in safety with confidence,
knowing that the virtues of my heart,
will lead me to the right decision.*

30 Gifted by the Fire of the Sun

Good Fortune is Supported
Through Commitment to the Wise use of Time

It is within the true nature of fire
to consume the fuel and move on.

Fire cannot exist without a source of fuel to cling to.

The sun and moon cling to heaven,
the grass and trees cling to earth.

Fire in the morning,
the sun awakens all living things,
thus, the day begins.

The community clings to the wise use of time.

Fire in the evening,
do not yield to lamenting that time has passed.

Be flexible in compliance with the ways of nature.

As the sun sets the wise prepare for rest,
avoiding the temptation
to burn low the life force through revelry.

When the brightness of the day withdraws
the light of the moon penetrates the darkness.

Fire Above - Fire Below

The Clarity of the Light is Reflected Within the Self

Fire has no definite form
but clings to the source,
and thus, is bright.
Our life is defined
by what we cling to.

Your recognition of limitations
depends on your understanding
of the forces of the universe.

The light of clarity within
depends on strict adherence
to conformity with that which is correct.

The outcome depends on
what you value and the actions of the day.

Clarity of purpose is the source of your prosperity.

FIRE
As I stand in the light of the day,
I am warmed by the fire gifted by the sun.
The light within is my fire, gifted at birth.
As the day ends, I prepare for rest,
to restore and nurture the source of my life's force.

31 The Influence of Mutual Attraction

Good Fortune to Those who Have the Patience
To Consider Carefully Before Acting

The balance of mutual attraction
reveals the true nature of relationships.

The stillness of the mountain influences the lake
to return to the tranquility within the earth.

The creative seeks the receptive,
opposites attract, uniting a relationship is formed.

The glow of the moon influences the darkness.

The sun shines and the cold of the night withdraws.

The wind blows
bringing the nurturance of rain to the land.

Through the ages a path has formed
to surrender the overflow of the lake
to the caverns beneath the mountain.

The mutual influence
of sun and moon, wind, and rain,
fills the fields with the harvest of summer.

As winter approaches
the tranquility of prosperity unifies the people.

Mutual attraction influences
the people to care about each other.

Lake Above - Mountain Below

The Lake Dwells Within the Cradle of the Mountain

The balance of yin and yang.
In nature all things
belong to heaven and earth.
Through the influence,
of the power of attraction,
there is fulfillment.

Life on earth evolves
through the involuntary responses of the heart.

The tranquility of the heart
inspires the fulfillment of balanced energies.

Like all who dwell upon the earth,
you are loved and cared for
by those who prepared your soul
to understand the nature of true love.

INFLUENCE
It is through the emptiness of an open heart,
and a quiet mind that I am willing
to yield to the influences of nature.
I do not rush forward seeking immediate satisfaction.
I persevere, seeing the way through contemplation,
to influence the hearts of my community.

32 The Continuity of Endurance

Good Fortune as the Magnetic and Dynamic
Forces Work Together to Endure

The eldest son of thunder moves through the land,
arousing the eldest daughter of the wind,
they travel together unconcerned.

Unhindered they move freely
with no beginning and no end.

It is within the nature of heaven and earth
for all things to organize for survival.

The dynamic force of thunder inspires,
and shocks as change is on the horizon.

The gentleness of the wind endures
through unconditional perseverance to a fixed direction.

In the lives of the people, the gentle and the strong
establish relationships that are capable of duration,
through devotion to eternity.

The duration of time passing,
and the constancy of change are eternal.

With firmness of character,
and perseverance there is unity.

Through the understanding
of that which always is there is success.

Through the duration of time the course of eternity is set.

Thunder Above - Wind Below

The Symmetry of Thunder and Wind

Dynamic forces of change.
The perpetual motion
of expansion and contraction
endures the passage of time.

32 ENDURANCE

The force of continuous change does not effect
the consistency of the sun and the moon.

The dynamic and magnetic are eternal,
with every ending there is a new beginning.

The consistent commitment
to the secrets of eternity
are manifest within the self.

Standing firm with a fixed direction
penetrates the winds of change through perseverance.

Through the internal organization of self,
the duration of relationship is guaranteed.

ENDURANCE
At times I am tossed about,
by the inevitable imposition of the external.
As I face the challenges of transformation,
I renew my commitment to that which endures.
It is the constancy of strength within that prevails.

33 Retreat to Freedom

Good Fortune to Those who Recognize
The Time to Quietly Withdraw

This is the time for a strategic retreat
to avoid being drawn into an undesirable situation.

When the freedom to move forward is lost,
the wise avoid danger through cooperation.

It is natural for those in inferior positions
to challenge those in control.

True to their convictions the wise
do not take flight in the face of danger.

To remain free, a successful retreat
relies on careful preparation and timing.

Strength, clarity, and good timing are essential,
as hostility advances the sage does not contend.

Quietly they wait
for the opportunity to withdraw voluntarily.

If through hesitation the danger has advanced,
it is best to remain still.

In this way small things can be achieved
until there is an opening to escape.

Focused and perseverant they attend to the daily
matters that sustain through difficult times.

Retreat to freedom unhindered by regret for what is lost.

Heaven Above - Mountain Below

The Mountain Reaches up to Heaven

The transformation from light to dark.
There is danger from adversity.
The sage withdraws
to seek the wisdom of the celestial ruler.

33 RETREAT

Assume an unwavering commitment to an internal retreat.

Bide your time, by adjusting your mind,
set in motion the willingness to withdraw to safety.

Remain outwardly cheerful until the time is right
to remove yourself from the situation.
At the first opportunity to carry out
a countermove, the decision will not be difficult.

Those who are left behind will not succeed on their own.
There is no blame, it is good to have somewhere to go.

When all else fails, lead the way for those you cherish.

RETREAT
Resisting the demand of subtle dangers
I take no action.
Through experience I have learned
to prepare for the unexpected.
To assure success I quietly withdraw to safety.
I contemplate retreat, no matter the cause.
Trusting my desire to be safe,
I remain comfortable in my place.

34 Old Goat Does Not Yield

Good Fortune to Those who do not
Rely on Force to Achieve Their Goals

The old goat, self-righteous in the ways of the past,
uses force to gain advantage.

Unconscious of the great power of the times,
he resists the opportunity to be led.

Resisting constraint, he butts his head
against the hedge and becomes entangled.

Once entangled, unable to move forward or backward,
his obstinate disposition must yield.

When the old goat grows weary, unable to achieve
his goals he withdraws, seeking his proper place.

For the people, resistance, and obstruction,
toward what is right leads to remorse.

To advance, those who do not wait
for the right time will surely encounter danger.

With perseverance, which does not degenerate into force,
one remains unhindered.

Misuse of power relents, as the balance
of decrease and increase swings to a new beginning.

True greatness invigorates potential.
Remain centered in moderation.

Thunder Above - Heaven Below

Thunder Invigorates the Creative Power of Heaven

34 POWER

The great strength of creation
is inspired by the power of movement.
Moderation tempers the will.
Remain centered
in the magnetic use of force.

This is a time to remain true
to the fundamental principles of appropriate actions.

Like the obstinate goat, to move forward
with great force risks entanglements.

When faced with resistance
do not push ahead regardless of circumstances.

To achieve great influence be resolute
in your willingness to do what is right.

In good time regret withdraws,
obstacles give way as the worthy persist.

POWER
Awaiting the union of movement through strength,
I am challenged by the impulse to take an action.
I do not force the issue.
I persevere, knowing with certainty,
that I will not hesitate to make the necessary changes
when the time is right.

35 The Advance of Consciousness

The Good Fortune of Effective Leadership
Depends on the Loyalty of Those who Follow

The mists of the dawn linger,
clinging to the shelter of the stillness of the night.

As the sun rises above the earth,
the purity of its light shines down upon all things.

The primordial yin force,
of the feminine principle, is in the place of power.

To attain happiness
one must have the perseverance of the ancestress.

Through the feminine principle of persistence,
the influence of the queen mother,
brings good fortune to the sorrows of the king.

Once misunderstandings are cleared up,
those of like mind, joining together, move forward.

The king rewards those who serve to advance.

Those who dwell in darkness withdraw
as the radiant light of dawn imposes.

The virtue of clarity prevails
within a society that is ruled by wisdom and justice.

The enlightenment of the people is acknowledged.

Like the brightness of the light
there is clarity in the power of self-awareness.

Fire Above - Earth Below

The Light of the Sun Rises Above the Earth at Dawn

35 ADVANCE

*The light of the enlightened
shines from within.
Through clarity
the course is set for advancement.*

It is the wisdom of the feminine
to avoid mistakes through stillness.

When there is no confidence
to support your goals,
remain calm and composed.

When your position is weak
it is wise to stand still and wait for a clear path.

Throughout history progress advanced by cooperation.

Seek help from those who serve
from the principle of self-awareness.

Clarity from within transforms the darkness into light.

ADVANCE
*Be conscious of danger.
Do not wander into humiliation.
Sorrow is not necessary, there is always gain and loss.
Do not lose heart, nor be dependent on external things.
Remain true to the light,
and progress will surely follow.*

36 The Tyrant is on the Border

*Good Fortune to Those Whose Actions
are in Accord with Their Circumstances*

Throughout history the multitudes have rejected tyranny.

In times of darkness
those who are enlightened prefer to withdraw,
knowing that the light that dwells within,
cannot be extinguished.

Conditions were such that the feudal lords
of the Zhou Dynasty were unable to expand
to the south without resistance at the borders.

The tyrant of Shang, true only to his personal interests,
prepares his armies to defend the borders of his kingdom.

Resisting his orders his princes,
and lords stood in terror of his wrath.

When those in authority are of a dark nature
the gentle light within must yield.

To avoid the severity of imprisonment
they retreated into hiding.

Seeking safety from the revenge,
of King Shang by hiding in the bushes they escaped,
by joining the legions of the encroaching clans.

*To be in a strong position
at the right time requires a clear intention.*

Earth Above - Fire Below

The Brilliance of the Sun
Sinks Into the Shadow of the Earth

36 DARKNESS

As the sun sinks beneath the horizon
there is awareness of danger.
In the darkness of night
the light of the sun remains hidden.

This is a time to maintain a clear focus
on your own values and goals.

Through adversity, persevere,
while quietly retreating to evade the issues.

Just as the sun yields to darkness,
it is certain that the light will emerge again.

Those who lead, and those who follow,
will sow the seeds of the future.

DARKNESS
In times of adversity
I am aware of the danger.
When confronted by those
who could wound me,
I am cautious.
As I contemplate my situation,
I maintain a clear focus,
on the power of my intention.

37 All for One and One for All

To Invite Good Fortune
Now is the Time to Support Those of Like Mind

The power to influence is hidden
within the ways of the family.

A well-formed structure, of a functional family,
establishes the rules of good conduct.

In society the alliance within the family follows tradition.
Each person represents the fulfillment
of correct conduct within the community.

It is the tradition within most societies around the world,
that the eldest male is responsible for the family,
as it relates to outside the home.

The eldest female is responsible
for the relationships within the home.

The relationship between the husband,
and wife holds the family together.

Appropriate enforcement of rules,
within the home, sets the foundation for conformity.

In this way a strong and stable kinship is established.

Kinship, the perseverance of those who support,
influences loyalty for those who lead.

Order within the community
fuels relationships around the world.

That which is within influences that which is without.

Wind Above - Fire Below

The Fire Fuels the Survival of the Wind

37 FAMILY

The gentleness of the wind
moves freely about, seeking nothing.
The fuel of the fire feeds the wind
which influences the path
of good fortune.

Just as the direction of the wind is influenced
by the fuel of the fire, be gentle in your ways.

No longer are you constrained
by the ancient rules of relationship traditions.

Look within, what is the fuel that fans your fire?

Where and how are you willing to conform?

There is a place within your community
that supports your dreams.

FAMILY
Regardless of gender, within every family,
there are those who lead
and those who follow.
The patriarchal societies of the past,
have given way to variables of traditional roles.
It is those who support,
through perseverance and loyalty,
that those who lead,
are able to focus on productivity.

38 Alone on the Path of Opposition

Good Fortune to Those who see the Situation
as an Opportunity to Seek New Awareness

The independence of all that exists,
survives in response to the universal laws of nature.

Just as fire rises, and water descends.
Humanity coexists through
the magnetic attraction of opposites.

The second sister, energy rising, the nature of fire,
opposes the third sister, energy descending,
the nature of water stored in the lake.

The viewpoints of two sisters diverge,
yet they do not attempt to enforce their opinions.
To move forward with force would empower distrust.

If open hostility lingers,
each remains true to her own nature.
When hindered by goals that would harm,
they each resort to small changes.

It is not by standing alone
in the face of opposition, that leads to resolution.

The willingness of joining together,
to resolve misunderstandings invites success.

Small steps build the bridge to reconciliation.
The principle of opposites transcends obstruction.

The reconciliation of individual differences
enables the power of eternity through clarity of union.

Fire Above - Lake Below

Fire and Water go Their Own Ways

38 TRANSCEND

*The transcendence of opposition
nurtures creation.
Those who are estranged by
misunderstandings, soon return.*

Even though fire and water can destroy each other,
it is their nature to coexist.

This is a time to submit to those who have the strength
to disperse your concerns and restore peace.

Join with persons of like mind to establish
the definition of what needs to be done.

That which is yours, when surrendered,
will return to you in good time.

TRANSCEND
*There are times when I am aware
that my opinions and goals
are in opposition,
to the standards of my community.
When those who oppose are strong, I remain soft.
Through that which I oppose
I seek the will to reconsider,
knowing that my willingness to compromise
leads the way to the path for resolution.*

39 The True Value of Adversity

Persistence on the Path of Good Fortune
Leads to the Cultivation of Self-Awareness

Travelers are stalled, bogged down
by the danger of uncertainty, many will turn back.

Those who persevere move haltingly
as they endure the difficulties of the unknown.

The mountain is steep and strong.
It is the nature of the mountain to remain still.

Unaware of its hindrance to progress,
it captures the rain within the craters of the ridge.

The power of the water,
greater than the strength of the mountain,
seeks a way to return to its home beneath the earth.

Through accumulation it finds a way
to trickle along the streams of the past.

In the village there is a woman who desires to walk,
but is only able to limp. Though she is afflicted,
she proceeds haltingly in her effort to achieve her goal.

To partecipate in society
she joins those who, are able, to assist.

With determination she chooses
to walk along the path of those who have gone before.

This is the time to observe the difference between
internal obstruction and external obstruction.

Water Above - Mountain Below

The Water in the Lake at the Crest of the Mountain

39 ADVERSITY

*When there is nowhere to go
the danger of obstruction
is worthy of respect.
In the face of adversity,
perseverance and self-reflection
inspire good fortune.*

The true value of adversity is the revolution within.

Steadfast pursuit of a goal eventually leads to an impasse.

In the face of hardship, when there is no easy way,
it is wise to pause at the first sign of trouble.

Do not press forward into uncertainty,
remain still and seek the wisdom within.

When there is no opportunity to advance,
it is best to resist the willingness to struggle.

ADVERSITY
*When I cannot succeed on my own,
I am aware that it would be reckless to proceed.
When the task is beyond my ability,
I seek the guidance of those who will assist.
Only in service to a higher cause,
through strength of spirit do I proceed,
in the face of danger.*

40 Return to Stability

Good Fortune to Those Who Attain the Middle Way

Thunder on the horizon notifies.
As the storm builds the atmospheric pressures increase.

Creating tension, electricity, generated by thunder
awakens movement in the heavens.

Thunder rattles, as the storm approaches
the tension in the clouds liberates, there is rain.

When there is nowhere to go,
time is taken to contemplate the situation.

The villagers are aware of the value
of what is great and what is small.

At the end of a storm, they quietly look about.
The air is fresh with hope on the horizon.

If there is somewhere to go, they hasten to assure success.

Life returns to normal as the buds of spring awaken.

As the chaos of extreme tension passes, regrets are released.

Offenders are forgiven and the work is resumed.

This is the time to set aside the attachment
to the causes of instability within the community.

Liberation as cooperation relieves the peril of chaos.

Thunder Above - Water Below

Thunder Liberates the Rain

40 STABILITY

Thunder brings rain,
tension is released.
The air has cleared.
Danger and obstructions
are resolved as the storm passes.

Take measure of yourself, there is no blame.

In your daily life, it is tension that generates movement.
The stimulation of constant movement leads to exhaustion.

When the time is right,
return to normal as quickly as possible.

Allow mistakes and misunderstandings
to yield to forgiveness.
Resist the temptation to carry your burdens forward.

Deliver yourself to the joys of life, love, and friendship.

STABILITY
You respond by seeking solutions,
yet you may not know the way.
Look within.
Be aware of good timing before you commit.
Look without.
Dissolve what you cannot tolerate.
Look around.
Who are your trusted companions?
Within you there is the power to embrace stability.

41 Ten Pairs of Tortoise Shells

Good Fortune Blends the Harmonious Balance
of Service Without Sacrifice

Game, fish, tortoise, and turtles were abundant
in the regions around the Yellow River Valley.

The shells of the tortoise and the turtle
became valuable, as there was a demand for divination.

At the end of the day the people gathered,
telling stories around the fire and nourishing themselves.

Bones and shells were tossed into the fire,
to create these valuable cracks as well.

Heated sticks were used to cause unique cracking patterns.
The patterns provided the answer to a question.

There came a time when society established a system
for the valuation of property.

Fortune telling, to seek advice from the ancestors,
became the privilege of the king.

Ten pairs of tortoise shells were given to the king.

Ceremonies were performed to transfer wealth
from the people to the ruling class.

The people demanded reciprocation for what is given,
and what is received in return.

If the wealth of the community is sacrificed
to enrich the unworthy, the system will fail.

Mountain Above - Lake Below

As the Lake Evaporates into the Mist
the Mountain Grows Greener

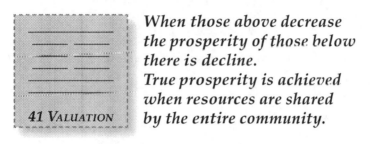

When those above decrease
the prosperity of those below
there is decline.
True prosperity is achieved
when resources are shared
by the entire community.

41 VALUATION

The I Ching was documented by scholars, to create
a source of divination as a form for written language.

There are great rewards
as the balance of harmony is maintained for all.

Those in power,
and those who serve must support each other,
as neither can exist without the other.

When you are in a position of power, be generous.

VALUATION
In times of prosperity,
I consider carefully, how much to give
to those who may be able
to survive without assistance.
Through simplicity,
I gain the strength for what is needed,
to strive forward without suffering.

42 The Liberation of Opportunity

*Supreme Good Fortune
to Those who Accomplish Great Deeds*

New opportunities emerge as sustainable
agriculture establishes the value of common goals.

28th century BCE, the use of wood to create tools
for cultivation, established awareness of intention.

The clan of the Divine Husbandman

The mythical emperor Shen Nong invented
the wooden plow to loosen the soil for cultivation.

His catalog of medicinal plants became
the basis of theory for Traditional Chinese Medicine.

By taming the ox and horse
he taught the people to clear the land with fire.

In this way the creativity of one man
increased the well-being of humanity for all time.

Teachers and inventors, who manifest what is needed,
increase the stability of the community.

Even though ancient cultures designated and supported
ruling families, it was those who increased the well-being,
of all the people, that were truly powerful.

*When those in power are aware, of the needs
of the common people, there is progress for all.*

Wind Above - Thunder Below

Wind and Thunder Inspire the True Will of the Self

42 OPPORTUNITY

The powers of wind and thunder work together to increase each other. When leaders embrace the needs of the people balance spreads across the land.

The seeds of progress lay beneath the soil,
waiting for the comfort of spring.

As the sprout emerges from darkness
toward the light there is the promise of prosperity.

Wind and wood represent slow gentle movement.

When conditions are right, mutual support
manifests the opportunity for new beginnings.

The harmony of self-awareness,
supports good fortune, for those who are willing
to contribute to the needs of others.

OPPORTUNITY
*The rituals of change support me,
as I endure the limits of darkness.
Commitment to daily progress is central.
In times of increase new opportunities emerge.
Investing my awareness in what is useful,
I spend my time enjoying the gentleness
of my faith in creation.*

43 The Power of One

*Good Fortune to Those who
are Forearmed in the Face of Danger*

Clouds form, reaching up to heaven.

True to the justice of the universe,
the rain enriches all things.

When the accumulation of tension,
exceeds its potential for benefit, there is danger.

The city must be notified.

One calls out, to make the matter known to the king.
He walks alone through the rain, there is no blame.

Within the village there are those who would
take advantage of difficult situations.

In the face of danger, it is wise to be prepared.

The court follows the teaching of the sage,
selfless commitment to kindness for all.

Dikes and channels are built to control
the rivers that caused destruction in the past.

In this way harmony, and a sense well-being
will spread throughout the community.

Independence supports security.

*The virtues of goodness, and cooperation,
disperse fears and generate self-respect.*

Lake Above - Heaven Below

The Wealth of the Lake Supports the Creations of Heaven

43 One

*In nature gathering is always
followed by dispersion.
The lake ascends to heaven forming
the accumulation of clouds.*

The lake represents the distribution of wealth.

When those at the top are of weak character,
there is no one to call.

Without the support
of those below they will surely stand alone.

It takes only one goat to destroy the garden.

Be firm in your awareness, do not pity
those who cause trouble in the dark of the night.

43 POWER OF ONE
*I seek awareness of what I am holding onto.
Even though there are dangers all around,
I know that there are ways
to be of service to my community.
The traumas and hardships of my past,
are resolved by my commitment to self-respect,
and the power of my independence.*

44 The Magnetic Attraction of Temptation

Good Fortune to Those who
Understand the Value of Constraint

In the month of June, at the summer solstice,
the increase of summer begins to yield to decline.

As the prosperity of summer declines there are things
to be done, the people begin to adapt to the inevitable.

The prince travels throughout the region,
he takes interest in what is happening in his kingdom.

He seeks to encounter a wife
that does not challenge his authority.

Knowing that a man should not be tempted to marry
a strong woman, he withdraws, aware of the inevitable
fate of being dominated for the rest of his life.

Friends and family cannot influence,
as the temptation of mutual attraction inspires action.

The unworthy, when unrestrained,
soon grow to a force that is capable of raging about.

The influence of poor character must be constrained
to support the well-being of the many.

When making choices he seeks out only those,
who are willing to meet him halfway?

To influence his intention,
he remains free to respond through correct action.

The judicious deter the potential for harm.

Heaven Above - Wind Below

The Wind Blows Beneath Heaven

44 *ATTRACTION*

*It is fundamental that magnetic
attraction rules the world.
The power of nature supports
creation for the renewal of life.*

In the spring the wind blows
across the surface of the earth.

Tempting fate, the seeds of the future
ride on the wind, seeking their destiny.

The magnetic attraction of the inevitable,
supports the circumstances required to fulfill their destiny.

The power of magnetic attraction invites your destiny.
Seeking union with others, be cautious in your approach.

The sweetness of the melon ripens slowly,
hidden beneath the shade of the leaves,
protected by the wisdom of its ancestors.

ATTRACTION
*Be aware of the intensity of temptation.
Do not be the one
that must be constrained.
Adapt to the changes demanded by the times.
When the magnetism of heaven and earth join,
the power of attraction is engaged for all.*

45 Cause and Effect

Good Fortune as the People Celebrate
With Devotion to Common Goals

An individual drop of rain gathers to form a lake.
As the rain collects, it soon becomes a powerful force.

When the danger of such a force is anticipated,
it is necessary to channel the weight of the water.

In anticipation of the unexpected,
the dangers are deflected through preparation.

The king returns to the temple to prepare an offering.

Strong leaders, supported by mutual respect,
unify their commitment to the future.

Gathering tools to defend the village,
the assemblage of unified communities set forth.

Through conformity a congregation is formed,
creating a united legion of followers.

When organized society
enforces conformity within the ranks,
the gathering of power effects
the independence of future generations.

The demands of nature
enforce the sacrifice of independence
through the value of mutual benefit.

To understand the demands of cause and effect
Now is the time to be prepared for the inevitable.

Lake Above - Earth Below

Heaven and Earth Join, and the Work of Life Begins

45 GATHERING

At the beginning of all things
there must be more than one.
The natural occurrence
is for all creatures to gather.

Birds flock, insects swarm, mammals gather.
Relationships are formed for the sake of survival.

The masses of humanity unite
through the centralization of belonging.

To meet another with joy and devotion
is the beginning of a relationship.

There is a danger, that devotion to the unworthy,
will establish a force to which you cannot conform.

It is conformity through devotion to purpose that endures.

GATHERING
If your community has lost
its reverence for the forces of nature,
do not lose your way as you stand alone.
In resistance to leadership,
that ceases to serve the people,
stand united with the natural laws
of cause and effect.

46 Welcome to the World

Good Fortune as Many Small Things
are Accomplished Through Devotion to the Goal

Rooting down into the earth,
the little tree grows strong as it reaches for the sky.

In this way the energies are balanced and the future
is set through commitment to gradual increase.

This is a time of favorable conditions for transformation.

Like-minded people in power are able
to clear obstructions for projects that benefit all.

Those of good nature push through
the myriad of small things with confidence.

The modest set to work, devoted to the project.
Through adaptability success is assured.

In society, to rise from a low position,
you must be grounded through solidarity within yourself.

It is the way of the world
to grow through the efforts of many small steps.

In favorable times progress is achieved
through commitment to those who work together.

Earth Above - Wood Below

The little tree reaches upward
from its shelter within the Earth

46 WELCOME

A great effort is required,
to advance from the roots,
to achieve the outcome.
Like the gradual growth of the tree,
achievements are gained,
through slow steady progress.

This is a time to position yourself for a favorable response.

Like the seed which emerges only when the time is right,
your goals are supported
by opportunities that ensure your growth.

As you move forward, be devoted to who you are
with sincerity, and loyalty to your goals.

Coordinate your emotions with clear thinking.

Seek out that which contributes
to your happiness and well-being.

WELCOME
Carefully planning, the goals I wish to achieve,
I approach only those with interests in similar projects.
When I am able, to support others,
I choose those who demonstrate a willingness
to persevere through calm steady progress.

47 Spare the Word Strengthen the Back

Through Inner Stability, Despite all Dangers,
There is the Promise of Good Fortune

The strength of the mountain
supports the abundance of the lake.

If the mountain is unstable the lake drains.

Descending to the caverns with the earth.
Even though the ability to fulfill its purpose has failed,
the mountain remains still.

This is a time when unusual circumstances
impose disruption through the unexpected.

The strong of spirit persevere, though exhausted,
they quietly resist the danger of surrender.

Times of adversity impose constraints.

The progress, of those who are willing to accomplish
their goals, no matter the consequences of obstruction.

Those who choose to lead must be supported
by those who understand he laws of nature.

When surrounded by inferior people,
strong leaders remain calm and cheerful.

It is the fear of exhaustion that awakens
intention finds the way to be truly free of oppression.

Lake Above - Water Below

The Invisible Power of Stillness Within

Confinement imposed
by the instability of oppression.
Adversity does not bend
those whose power is within.

47 OPPRESSION

At this time, be prepared to meet difficulty with confidence.

Remain still when surrounded
by those who are restless and uncertain.

Be stable in the face of danger,
to push ahead despite adversity invites disgrace.

Obstructions from without
are best handled by the invisible powers within.

When there is no one to listen, there is no need to speak.

OPPRESSION
I do not bend to that which constrains.
Trusting in the power of stability within,
I find consolation in the strength of stillness.
When there is nowhere to go
I endure through joy and celebration.

48 The Unchangeable Within Change

*Good Fortune Depends
on a Clear Connection to Self-Awareness*

The wealth of pure water is hidden beneath the earth.

The wealth of the community depends
on a reliable source of pure water.

When the water is not pure there is work to be done.

There was much coming and going as the people
replenished themselves from the pure water of the well.

The well, in the center, belongs to the king.

Over the course of centuries politics and dynasties changed.

The style of buildings also changed
but the well remained connected to its source.

There came a time when the village must move
to take advantage of more favorable conditions.

They set to work to establish a new well, the bottom and
sides of the well are tiled to protect the clarity of the water.

Divisions of the land surrounding are defined.

Ceremonies were held in the temples of the ancestors
to encourage the loyalty of the people.

*The cultivation of good character depends
on a continuous flow of wisdom from within.*

Water Above - Wood Below

The Wood draws Water From the Well

48 THE WELL

Wood, the symbol of spring.
New growth transforms water
into nourishment.
The needs of the people,
who draw from the well,
are eternal and do not change.

Like the inexhaustible clarity of the well,
your life source must be free of stagnation.

If the rope, which draws the water
to the surface is broken, there is misfortune.

Be aware that your heart is the center of your reality.

Even though change is upon you,
remain true to the purity of wisdom from within.

In times of change be committed to your strength within.

Encourage others to organize in ways that benefit the whole.

THE WELL
Like the well, my inner wealth is stationary.
It is my intention to dwell within a social structure,
that leads the way to the well of good fortune for all.
I draw from the clear source of the unchangeable.

49 The Universal Experience of Reckoning

Through the Desire for Mutual Benefit,
Small Changes Lead to Good Fortune

Like the constancy of the passing of time,
nature protects all life through adaptation.

In politics revolution arises
when opposite forces are causing stagnation.

When those in power are weak,
their influence destroys that which benefits the majority.

The time has come to calculate the demands,
of the those who serve, the people.

When those who subdue each other
are challenged, they must seek the middle way.

A person of goodwill and integrity,
with the correct support, is needed to re-assure the people.

When there is no other way, preparations must be made.

When the time is right new leadership
establishes a legitimate system of justice.

An agreement with the goals of the new leadership
is put in place and announced to all.

By avoiding extremes
the people conform to the new ways,
and life goes on.

With awareness of the passing of time.
The wise set their calendar in order.

Lake Above - Fire Below

The Equal Forces of Fire and Water

49 RECKONING

The lake above the fire below.
Both have the power
to destroy the other.
In times of reckoning
that which no longer serves
is released without regret.

As the seasons change the animal's pelt
transforms in response to the new conditions.

To do away with what is no longer needed,
invites the miracle of renewal.

Are you stuck in a system that no longer serves you?

When your day comes, will you be ready
to start a revolution within yourself.

Is this the time for you to reckon
with what is holding you back?

Now is the time to discover
your own creative development.

RECKONING
There are times when my way is blocked by conflict.
Forces that impede my progress,
may require perseverance to achieve my goals.
I adapt, knowing that I will make
the necessary changes when the time is right.

50 Fan the Flame of a New Beginning

Great Good Fortune to Those who
Nourish the Flame and Honor the Spirit

The bronze age, and the evolution of religion,
brought refinement to civilization.

The Ting is a cauldron made of bronze,
which was revered in the temples of the ancestors.

It represents nourishment
through the correct placement of resources.

The sacred vessel was treasured as an heirloom.

The prince turns the Ting upside down.

When there is stagnation, the Ting is cleaned
in preparation for a new beginning.

When a new dynasty was established,
the first declaration was to cast a new ting,
and inscribe the constitution on it.

The joining together of communities
through celebration allowed progress.

Joint efforts of leaders, who work in harmony,
establish a home where the basic needs
of the people are contained.

With humility through sacrifice,
and nourishment of the worthy there is enlightenment.

Fire Above - Wood Below

Wood Provides the Fuel to Nourish the Fire

The wind fans the flame
yet the fire cannot stand alone.
Transformation
supported by wind
nourishes the worthy.

The spirit is fueled by the nourishment of faith.

Consolidate your fate by placing yourself
in the correct position for success.

Turn your beliefs upside down,
and shake out what is causing stagnation.

Find the way to consolidate what is needed
to abolish old habits that no longer serve.

Much can be accomplished through
the reinforcement of your faith in transformation.

BEGINNING
I fan the flames of my dreams and desires.
My value is recognized by my companions.
I have faith in honoring myself and others.
Through perseverance my position is safe,
as I celebrate to invoke the fate of good fortune.
The visible grows beyond itself and becomes invisible

51 Shake Rattle and Roll

Good Fortune Returns
Renewed Commitment to Joy and Laughter

When thunder roars the earth rattles,
arousing fear far and wide.

Startled by the thunder
the frightened creatures run about hither and dither.

The people respond, fearing God,
they abandon their tasks and head for the hills.

Great leaders remain composed,
knowing that the fear of God is beneficial.

When the danger has passed,
they withdraw to avoid blame.

Without resources, unable to resist the change,
they return home with new awareness.

With reverence they set their lives in order,
knowing that what is lost can be replaced.

Celebrations are arranged to restore faith,
and inspire action through joy and laughter.

The people are refreshed
as tension is released and life goes on.

External threats do not have the power to weaken
the foundation of your time-honored traditions

Thunder Above - Thunder Below

The Shock of Thunder Revives the Weary

51 SHOCK

Arousing terror and fear.
Thunder rolls across the plains.
Shock and danger prevail.
The enlightened remain reverent.

Thunder in the spring represents
the transformation of future generations.

New leaders establish reforms.
and the business of governing is renewed.

When you are faced with shocking situation,
remain calm, even when you must move
to higher ground for safety.

SHOCK
When my world is rattled by shock and fear,
I am protected by my faith in the future.
Through preparation for the inevitable,
I am awakened to new possibilities.
When the time comes to act, I follow my plan,
assisting others along the way.

52 When There is Nowhere to Go

Good Fortune to Those who Honor
the Importance of Silence

Stopping at the foot of the mountain,
we take time to contemplate the journey ahead.

Unanticipated conditions have delayed our progress.

Knowing that we must stop there is no blame,
we cannot go on forever without rest.

Taking no action, we remain safe,
taking care of the needs of the present situation.

Eventually the willingness to struggle
withdraws allowing the mind to be calm.

Through the mystery of stillness,
the outside world does not impose.

We are safe in our stillness.

The inspiration of acceptance instills harmony,
opening the path to a quiet heart.

The Taoist principal of keeping still
assumes a complement of energies within.

The calmness of the heart inspires
the transformation of confusion to peace of mind.

Experience and intuition understand
and regulate our needs.

Mountain Above - Mountain Below

Stillness at the Foot of the Mountain

52 STILLNESS

*At the beginning there is harmony
within the heart of the mountain.
It is the natural order of creation
to honor the time for rest.*

Through the mystery of stillness,
the outside world does not impose.

Look within, your heart guides the way.

Standing still, imagine your feet knowing where to go,
your knees, willing to bend.

Strengthen your waist,
be willing to be open to new ways.

Through firmness and truth,
with the support of your intuition, remain resolute.

Choose your words carefully and there will be no regrets.

Eventually the willingness to struggle withdraws,
allowing the mind to be calm.

STILLNESS
*My path is guided by the awareness of eternity.
I do not seek the absolute,
I seek only balance and understanding through acceptance.
Knowing that the stillness of the universe,
and the natural laws of the cosmos, rule my actions.*

53 The Wild Goose Rides the Winds

Good Fortune to Those who
Lead the way to Abundance for all

The wild goose rides the wind,
seeking a place of nourishment and shelter.

True to its nature,
when it finds a suitable place,
it calls out announcing its desire to share the bounty
of the discovery in peace and tranquility.

In the sky two flocks of geese are circling.

Each flock has a strong leader.
It is a peaceful day; storm clouds are on the horizon.

They move neither north nor south but continue to circle.

Their calculations are flawless as they unite into one flock.

If a few fall behind, slowing the progress of all,
there is no blame.

Turning away from the storm,
they fly together at a pace that is suitable for all.

When the wild goose calls out,
their course turns toward the clear sky on the horizon.

The strong lead the way to establish
the norms that will last through generations.

The union of the weak and the strong
forms relationships of mutual support.

Wind Above – Mountain Below

The Course of Lasting Stability

53 STABILITY

*Wind gently penetrates
the stillness within the mountain.
Moisture from the wind
invites the seeds of last year's bounty
to emerge toward the light.*

Each day we choose when to lead and when to follow.

For humanity the formalities of relationship
are supported by the stability rooted in tradition.

With gentleness, dignity, and common virtues,
agreements progress along their natural course.

Joining together, we guide the way
to stabilize the course of the future.

Like the wild goose, we do not choose to stand alone.

LASTING STABILITY
*I cultivate the course of lasting stability.
The ways of nature support my ability to thrive.
Through adaptation, the evolution of life endures.
I celebrate my life with joy and ceremony,
wishing good fortune to those who dwell in gratitude.*

54 To Seek a Favorable Position

Good Fortune to Those who Establish
Agreements That are Fair to all Parties

It was the custom for the king to have only one wife.

Yet, beneath the appearance of order, there is discontent.

The little sister trembles in the presence of the king.

Seeking a favorable position, for the sake of survival,
she must yield to the established heritage of subordination.

Within the household the chain of command was clear,
the first to marry rules.

The discomforts of this arrangement
required her to submit to the demands of the first wife.

The initiation of second wives
as concubines, was a custom without ceremony.

Kings and lords were independent,
entitled to follow their own initiative.

Ceremonies of a formal marriage established
a relationship that endured through time.

Society formed around the leadership
of the descendants of the king.
In this way the kingdom was protected
through subordination to tradition.

The traditions of rank, and the clarity of agreements
within relationships ensures harmony and good will.

Thunder Above – Lake Below

Thunder Rolls Across the Lake
The Softness of the Water Trembles

54 Position

The cycle of life exists through
the transitional balance of energy.
To seek favorable conditions,
through subordination,
there is no blame.

This is the time to be clear in what you wish to achieve.

Through established contracts
the traditions of the past are re-enforced.

When those in powerful positions are unaware
of the suffering of those without options,
ceremonies and contracts secure relationships
that endure through time.

To advance your situation it is wise
to maintain your independence.

POSITION
To find myself in a position of subordination,
I need not allow the thunder
of authority to cause distress.
Seeking the opportunity to improve my situation,
I take care to make agreements that protect.
It is a society of independent adults who are able,
to support their families that enriches the world.

55 The Illumination of Awareness

Good Fortune to Those who Shield Themselves
From the Bewilderment of Ignorance

The sun, in its correct place in heaven at midday,
shines upon all things to fulfill its purpose.

Abundance in the summer brings forth
the crops for harvest in the fall.

With clarity of purpose
wise leaders encouraged the able bodied.

The efforts of those who are willing
to work together fulfill the goals of the community.
This required organization.

With awareness, and the intention for abundance,
they set forth to preserve the prosperity
of that which has been achieved.

For the people to be in their correct place,
there must be a place to call home.

An organized a system was established
for the rotation of crops according to the seasons.

In times of darkness,
it is the promise of the light, that sees one through.

Embrace the universal laws of balance
within the natural flow of increase and decrease.

What is central and correct will overcome
uncertainty through the power of illumination.

Thunder Above - Fire Below

Thunder Roars Lightning Strikes

The expansion of awareness
awakens the intention for abundance.
The sun at noon supports
the prosperity of increase and decline.

55 ABUNDANCE

To be truly free one must first have a clear heart.

To attain fullness, one must prepare for emptiness.

The phases of the moon
shine brightest just before they wane.

A highly evolved conception of your intention is required.

Awareness of the light within allows
the expression of the truth of your intentions.

To refrain from acting, is without blame,
when there is no hope of progress.

ABUNDANCE
In times of abundance,
I join with others to secure my future.
No matter the season,
I am grateful for what has been achieved.
It is the wisdom of the ancestors
that has taken me forward.
Now I am the ancestor.
It is time to prepare for the freedom of my children.

56 The Ways of the Wanderer

Mingling with Strangers
Humility Supports Good Fortune in Small Ways

When I see the fire on the mountain far above,
I know it is time to quietly go.

Even though I lose my home I yield to clarity and push on.

As I wander, I am a stranger to all.

Like the fire I seek new fuel,
a desire to move forward to discover new lands.

Attracting no attention, I am still, my strength is within.

Through stillness I succeed in small ways,
avoiding humiliation in a strange land.

Remaining cautious, I do not cling to the present moment.

Not wishing to engage with those who would harm me,
I do not linger but travel on, quietly passing through,
I submit to the strangeness of humanity.

Steadfastly I seek only to associate with good people.
I do not seek a new home until circumstances are favorable.

Bringing small gifts to gain new friends,
I reveal myself only when the time is right.

In times of transition, travelers take care to protect,
through attention to small matters.

Fire Above - Mountain Below

The Glow on the Horizon Inspires New Ways

56 WANDERER

Fire on the mountain,
the stillness of the mountain
does not yield.
The fire clings to the fuel of the land.
Its nature is to consume and move on.

At the foot of the mountain there is peace.
It is calm, I am stable.

Yet I see the fire above, I do not hesitate.

Through sacrifice and generosity
I gain the confidence of those who could help me.

When approaching new lands
I remain true to the guidance of what I observe.

I cling only to the stillness within, remembering,
there is a place where I belong.

THE WANDERER
In times of transition,
clarity and perseverance are my guides.
I stay on my path.
My good fortune is to cling only to the desire,
to understand the meaning of the times.

57 Go Gently Like the Wind

Good Fortune to Those
Who Comprehend Their Own Limitations

A favorable wind,
passing through the countryside,
invokes good fortune.

Those who wander set their intention
to assimilate into a more favorable situation.

They remain in the shadows,
undertaking only small matters they wait,
wishing to go unnoticed.

Crouching down, remaining safe,
they seek modest ways to adapt into a new community.

When the time is right, with humility,
they introduce themselves into the established society.

Those who seek to influence must understand
the goals and intentions of those who oppose.

Like the wanderer, seek to understand
the situation you wish to move into.

Through gentleness, the power of persuasion
penetrates the stagnation of the rigid.

To influence that which is strong
you must begin by being gentle with yourself.

Wind Above - Wind Below

Wind Follows Wind
The Gentle Influence of Perseverance

The grass must bend
to the will of the wind.
The ceaseless direction of intention
gently guides the way.

The wind blows gently across the surface of the earth.
The gentleness of the wind influences all things.

Restlessness and shame,
the repetition of the ways of inexperience,
lead to exhaustion.

The ceaseless direction of intention gently guides the way.
To influence that which is strong
you must begin by being gentle with yourself.

Set your intention to provide for yourself,
then to enjoy your good fortune.
Share your wisdom with others to influence the world.

GENTLY
I contemplate small ways to focus on my goals.
Waiting safely, I do not act until the time is right.
If my intention is to influence the outside world,
I must first clearly understand the nature of the times.
To penetrate that which has been established,
I appeal only those who have the power to create change.

58 The Animation of Joy

Good Fortune to Those Who Seek the Wisdom of the Sage

The babbling brook sings out joyfully,
inviting all creatures to gather in gratitude.

Joy and laughter, celebrated with others,
nurtures conformity to tradition.

Forgetting the drudgery of daily life,
the people happily submit to supporting each other.

Seeking those of like mind they congregate their efforts
to sustain through times of hardship.

If the desire for life to be easy
invites restlessness, some may lose their way.

Those who are self-indulgent,
lacking stability, will seek amusement.

There is concern that the stability,
of the goals of society, may be diverted.

The loss of control may challenge
what is firm and central for survival.

If celebration leads to distraction, misfortune soon follows.
Temptation and arrogance lead to remorse.

To trust in the illusions of self-indulgence
leads to the dispersion of purpose.

Excess revelry is like excess water
It must be controlled to avoid adversity.

Lake Above - Lake Below

The Joy of Inner Strength, Two Lakes Join Together

58 THE JOYOUS

*The intention to practice the lightness
of life, the will to sustain
through times of scarcity
animates the joy within.
The balance of nature supports life.*

Do not dwell on the ideal,
searching for the joy of a perfect world.

The balance in life is to walk the path of self-realization.

Lakes support rivers.
Lands embrace oceans.
Meadows create marshes.

Take comfort in the value of the goals
you have set for your life.
A quiet joy nourished from within
overcomes the confusion of inner conflict.

THE JOYOUS
*With joyous commitment to self and others,
I avoid the external dangers of excess.
As I study my dreams,
remorse disappears.
I animate the direction
I have set for my life,
Knowing that the essence
of true joy comes from within.*

59 The Dispersion of Stagnation

*Good Fortune as Hidden Grievances
are Dispersed Through Reconciliation*

The rain, purified by the wind,
scatters across the land,
enriching the lives of all things.

In winter, as ice forms,
the river becomes rigid and unyielding.

Even though rigidity obstructs,
the potential for progress remains within.

Like the water, which collects in the lake,
the people collect in communities.

The king makes plans,
temples of celebration are built,
and laws are established.

Religion is organized to break through,
and disperse divisive energies.

Rituals and sacred rights ensure
religious authority over the actions of the people.

Supported by joy and celebration, stagnation
is dispersed, releasing tension among the people.

Those whose vital energy is blocked
are healed through the gentleness of clarity.

*It is the nature of water to change in response
to the conditions of the seasons.*

Wind Above - Water Below

The Wind Transforms the Lake

59 DISPERSION

The wind blows gently across the lake,
dispersing the water into mist.
As clouds form accumulating tension,
there is rain and the return to peace.

The inexhaustible power
of transformation nourishes the future.

Hearts that are rigid are separated
from their community by ego.

When the constraints of ego exhaust progress,
they must be dispersed.

Those who have the courage
to dismiss the small can achieve the great.

In daily life the difficulties of the community,
must not become the difficulties of the self.

Through self-awareness the dispersion of ego,
allows you to return to peace within.

DISPERSION
Remaining vigilant in my self-awareness,
I do not exhaust myself through rigidity.
Yielding to harmony I disperse those who harms others.
In great challenges, I seek the wisdom of my ancestors.
Hoping that my commitments transform,
the awareness of true justice for future generations.

60 The Limitations of the Measure of Time

Good fortune to Those Who Move Forward
At the Right Time in the Right Place

Civilizations progressed within the boundaries of ideal
conditions for survival. To establish a home, one must
select a place with resources for the cultivation of crops.

Water is channeled to divert the possibility of flooding.

As communities expanded along the boundaries of the
Yellow River Valley, the power of an inexhaustible source
of water required adaptation to continuous change.

Wells are placed in the center of agricultural plots
which are assigned to family groups.

The year is divided into 24 periods
in anticipation of the impact of the passage of time.

Regulated periods of activity for domestic animals,
and farming were defined.

Once survival is secured, there is the issue
of establishing limitations for conduct.

Lawless hoarding, and stealing,
required the setting of limitations.

Rules of discretion, and boundaries
for the sharing of provisions, are set in place.

The measure of time passing.
Heaven and earth remain true to the rhythm of the universe.

Water Above - Lake Below

Regulation of the Power of Water

60 LIMITATIONS

The boundless energy of water
imposes awareness
of the forces of nature.
The natural limitations
of the seasons protect
from the excess of endless expansion.

Within the community laws and traditions
set limits as the foundation of justice.

In present time you witness the outcome
of these transitions, those in power cannot
impose excessive limitations on the people.

Awareness of the measure of time
enhances the prosperity of your limitations.

Be cheerful in times of peril,
recognizing the limits of your power to influence.

LIMITATIONS
In times of darkness, I surrender,
knowing that the light will soon return.
Recognizing the value of my own limitations,
I strengthen my ability to sustain the present.
Steadfastly I secure my resources.

61 The Inner Truth of an Open Heart

Good Fortune for Those
Who Approach the World Without Preconception

The course of humanity is altered through the
inner strength of sincerity. In ancient times
justice was guided by the principles of inner truth.

The Chinese character for truth
is the picture of a bird's foot over a baby chick.

To comprehend the I Ching
one must understand,
how the past influences the future.

Insurmountable obstacles are overcome,
by understanding without the bias of illusion.

To emerge into independence the budding of life,
depends on favorable conditions.

Troublesome people must be approached in the right way.

To gain power over intractable people,
one must first create a bond of trust, even thieves and
criminals work together with the power of common needs.

With sincerity and perseverance
the innocent can participate in the goals of the journey.

With the foundation of trust the fusion of strength,
and acceptance inspires self-confidence.

Wind Above - Lake Below

The Gentle Wind Blows Across the Surface of the Lake

The tranquility of the unconscious
is awakened to the forces of nature.
To understand the future requires
an open heart that is free of prejudice.

A firm foundation of trust unites the people
through gentleness and perseverance.

Time must be taken to establish a deep understanding
of the forces that surround you.

To influence your relationships
the inner truth of the situation must be set forth.

Center yourself in the ways of nature,
be gentle with what is not yet revealed.

Be open to your inner truth as you move forward.

Remain true to the balance of harmony within.

To understand the world you live in, leads to great success.

INNER TRUTH
The power of trust serves to harmonize society.
It is the correct attitude toward the outer world,
that cultivates independence through dependability.
A sincere heart, free of prejudice, is open to the truth.

62 The Small Bird Remains in Her Nest

*Good Fortune to Those Who Concentrate
on What can be Easily Achieved*

Thunder rumbles in the distance.
The storm is close to the land.

The small bird remains in her nest
until the time is right for her to fly.

If she flies before this time, she invites misfortune.

Knowing that there are times to act, and times to remain
still she quietly waits in safety for the storm to pass.

Like the stillness of the mountain,
she is not influenced by the actions of that which is beyond.

The approaching storm notifies the people
that difficult times are on the horizon.

Preparations for hardship are secured,
the wise to turn away from excessive actions.

Through the willingness to be satisfied
with small moves, danger is avoided.

When extraordinary conditions exist
only small things can succeed.

*Transition through small changes.
Proceed with modesty, the wise remain still
with reverence for extraordinary times.*

Thunder Above - Mountain Below

Thunder Lingers Above the Stillness of the Mountain

62 THE SMALL

Transition through small changes.
Proceed with modesty.
The wise remain still with reverence
for extraordinary times.

This is the time when excess action
has exceeded the boundaries of tradition.

Do not struggle when that which is strong
imposes its force upon you.

The soaring bird does not fly into the sun,
but returns to the safety of its home on the earth.

Remain devoted to the middle way
until things can be restored to normal.

Strive only to sustain your willingness
to commit to the power of humility.

In extraordinary times, intuition and,
good character will defend your belief in yourself.

THE SMALL
Taking no action, I am cautious.
Through modesty I am aware,
I do not exhaust myself to achieve nothing.
I reserve my strength with dignity,
and reverence for the conditions of the times.

63 The Instability of Coexistence

After Completion, as we Seek to Coexist,
Small Moves Support the Good Fortune of True Happiness

The powers of water and fire working together
in ways that avoid mutual destruction.

There is the instability of a new beginning.

Unseen dangers exist, and it is certain that they
will be revealed, by the powers of change.

The time is the 13th Century BC in China.

The emperor was titled "Illustrious Ancestor"
to honor the succession of the royal family.

The wars between the empire in the south,
and the Huns in the north resolved to colonialism.

Life without war resumed, however, there was the matter
of what to do with the unruly Huns.

Those who survived the wars must now be dealt with.

Even in peaceful times, to travel safely,
it was necessary to be well armed and on guard.

Despite the dangers, rules for expansion
through colonialism are established.

Correct behavior is integrated
into the present through ceremony and ritual.

It is foresight that prepares for the inevitable,
and arms against external actions.

Water Above – Fire Below

The Mutual Distress of Water Above Fire

63 COEXISTENCE

The transition from the old to the new reaches a point of completion.
When there is peace and tolerance, with appropriate precautions, hostile energies coexist.

Where there is order, there will disorder.
After completion of your goals
there are still matters to be dealt with.

When everything has been put in its correct place,
there is the potential for misfortune.

To plant the seeds of perfection
demands awareness of the laws of nature.
Remain in the correct place to ensure
the highest potential for progress.

Do not rest assuming that the goal has been achieved.

COEXISTENCE
*The instability of a new beginning, there will be the
temptation to relax and let things move forward.
As you settle into new surroundings,
and new routines, be aware that without concern
for details, you risk an uncertain outcome.
Arm yourself with wisdom from the course of history.
Coexist for the enjoyment of peaceful times.*

64 The Fox Crosses the River

Good Fortune as Opposites do not Occupy the Same Space

In ancient times the ways of the fox
served as the symbols of the folly and wisdom of nature.

The dilemma of the little fox, if her tail gets wet,
she cannot succeed in crossing the river.

If her tail freezes, she gets weighed down
by unforeseen circumstances.

The old fox understands how to cross the river.
She moves carefully alert to the danger.

With the promise of success,
she listens for signs of weakness in the ice.

Experience protects, she waits until the time is right.

With confidence she proceeds, moving forward,
she does not turn back but finds the way.

Not looking back, she proceeds
directly to the safety of the land beyond.

This is a moment of perfect balance,
which disperses into the awareness of a new beginning,

The completion of a journey as the past
becomes the present, and transitions into an open path.

*To cross the river without drowning
one must push forward without looking back.*

Fire Above - Water Below

Fire Dances boldly Across the Water

Powerful forces move in the direction
of what is true to their nature.
In times of transition,
it is the peace within,
that transforms the darkness into light.

64 COMPLETION

Fire and water are forces that can destroy each other.

To succeed, according to their nature,
they each must go their own way. By following their own
paths, their forces cannot influence the power of the other.

Before, you decide to move forward,
remember that all things must be in their proper place.

Do not exhaust yourself with actions against forces
that you cannot control, there is no success
without the correct attitude toward the unexpected.

Forethought and experience will guide you
to the completion of your goals.

COMPLETION
Success at the end of a long and tedious endeavor,
opens the way for transition and a new beginning.
To understand my own nature keeps me safe
as I travel along the winding rivers of my life.
There is the potential for success in every situation.

The Taoist Principle of Yin and Yang

The Perpetual Motion of Change

A reflection of the forces of change, as you set into motion,
the actions necessary to support change in your life.

For those who are unfamiliar with the I Ching

Instructions for tossing the coins,
and finding the hexagram are at the front of the book.

Focus on a concern that is occupying your thoughts.

For beginners, open the book and select a story at random.

Contemplate the story, especially the meditation.

Apply those thoughts to the situation of concern.

For those who are familiar with the I Ching and the changing lines

For the sake of simplicity there is no reference to the
traditional changing lines in the stories of this book.

Be aware of this moment and your intentions.

The author's choice is to encourage awareness,
and the importance of understanding the present situation.

If the intention is Yang, be aware of the moving force.

If the intention is Yin, be aware of the receptive force.

Yin attracts, Yang responds, the present changes to the future.

Good fortune to those who understand the ways of the world.

Asking Your Question

The Stories You Tell Yourself

Listen to your thoughts, is there a pattern that frequently
leads to a familiar outcome. Imagine the ideal.

Write down a question, whatever comes to mind.

Concerns that affect the lives of everyone:

You decide to do something but never seem to get around it.
An outside force blocks your progress.
The culture you live in doesn't reflect your beliefs.
You want to influence the people who
could support your goals.
Your intention is to be acknowledged
for your accomplishments.
You are considering a move or have
discovered a new interest.

These may be examples of the stories you are telling yourself.

The answers are revealed in the history, legends, and folklore,
of the divinations for people living in the 11th century BCE.

Stories were told as they migrated along the rivers,
and through the valleys of ancient China.

To seek the answer to your question,
you may find it helpful to contemplate
how the forces of nature reflect the times you are living in.

Good fortune to those who stand in the light of the truth.

The Forces of nature, the eight agents of change.
The influence of the story you tell yourself.

The Taoist Principle of Eternal Change

The time is the 11th Century, BCE

As night falls the people gathered around the fire
to inquire for guidance from the Divine.

The Changing Lines

Each story within the I Ching describes the unique
ways these ancient people prospered. The changing
lines indicate the possibilities as the present transforms
into the future. The 64 stories told here do not include
any reference to the changing lines. For simplicity
the author chooses to focus on the present situation,
emphasizing the importance of right action and the
good fortune within the story you tell yourself.

The Four Elements Theory, the Universal Forces of Nature

The elements of Air, Fire, Earth, and Water,
as they influence the lives of the people,
with the support of Heaven, Mountain, Lake, and Thunder.

The story offers a description of some
of the history of the times.
The subtitle refers to the influence of the natural
elements that represent the influence of those
two elemental forces upon each other.

It is the intention of the author to focus on the present.
Your situation and concerns at the time the question is asked.

To seek the answer to your question, you
may find it helpful to contemplate from the
perspective of the times you are living in.

*Good fortune to those who stand in the light of the truth,
taking responsibility for the story they tell themselves.*

Index

The Gift of Good Fortune   1

The Taoist Principle of Yin and Yang   6

The 8 Forces of Nature   7

1 Sage Rides Six Dragons to Heaven   8

Heaven Above - Heaven Below   9

2 The Receptive Earth   10

Earth Above - Earth Below   11

3 Enduring the Struggle to Emerge   12

Water Above - Thunder Below   13

4 The Influence of a Wise Teacher   14

Mountain Above - Water Below   15

5 Waiting for the Rain   16

Water Above - Heaven Below   17

6 Dilemma of the Arrogant Dragon   18

Heaven Above Water Below   19

7 The Discipline of a Peaceful Majority   20

Earth Above - Water Below   21

8 The Rivers of Your Destiny   22

Water Above - Earth Below   23

9 Gentle Winds Scatter the Clouds   24

Wind Above - Heaven Below   25

10 The Tail of the Tiger   26

Heaven Above - Lake Below   27

11 The Turning Point   28

Earth Above - Heaven Below   29

12 The Stagnation of Obstruction   30

Heaven Above - Earth Below   31

13 The Door is Open   32

Heaven Above - Fire Below   33

14 It Takes a Big Wagon   34

Fire Above - Heaven Below   35

15 To Cultivate Modesty Begin with the Heart   36

Earth Above - Mountain Below   37

16 The Joys and Mysteries of Life   38

Thunder Above - Earth Below   39

17 Those Who Lead Must Also Follow   40

Lake Above - Thunder Below   41

18 The Mistakes of the Past   42

Mountain Above - Wind Below   43

19 The Awakening of Spring   44

Earth Above - Lake Below   45

20 The King Contemplates the People   46

Wind Above - Earth Below   47

21 The Power of the Storm   48

Fire Above - Thunder Below   49

22 The Perfection of Grace   50

Mountain Above - Fire Below   51

23 The Opportunity of Misfortune   52

Mountain Above - Earth Below   53

24 A Glimmer of Light in the Darkness   54

Earth Above - Thunder Below   55

25 The Innocent Clarity of Intuition   56

Heaven Above - Thunder Below   57

26 The Nurturance of Prosperity   58

Mountain Above - Heaven Below   59

27 The Self Reliance of the Magic Tortoise   60

Mountain Above - Thunder Below   61

28 The Breaking Point   62

Water Above - Wood Below   63

29 Danger on The Path of Least Resistance   64

Water Above - Water Below 65

30 Gifted by the Fire of the Sun 66

Fire Above - Fire Below 67

31 The Influence of Mutual Attraction 68

Lake Above - Mountain Below 69

32 The Continuity of Endurance 70

Thunder Above - Wind Below 71

33 Retreat to Freedom 72

Heaven Above - Mountain Below 73

34 Old Goat Does Not Yield 74

Thunder Above - Heaven Below 75

35 The Advance of Consciousness 76

Fire Above - Earth Below 77

36 The Tyrant is on the Border 78

Earth Above - Fire Below 79

37 All for One and One for All 80

Wind Above - Fire Below 81

38 Alone on the Path of Opposition 82

Fire Above - Lake Below 83

39 The True Value of Adversity 84

Water Above - Mountain Below 85

40 Return to Stability 86

Thunder Above - Water Below 87

41 Ten Pairs of Tortoise Shells 88

Mountain Above - Lake Below 89

42 The Liberation of Opportunity 90

Wind Above - Thunder Below 91

43 The Power of One 92

Lake Above - Heaven Below 93

44 The Magnetic Attraction of Temptation 94

Heaven Above - Wind Below 95

45 Cause and Effect96

Lake Above - Earth Below97

46 Welcome to the World98

Earth Above - Wood Below99

47 Spare the Word Strengthen the Back100

Lake Above - Water Below101

48 The Unchangeable Within Change102

Water Above - Wood Below103

49 The Universal Experience of Reckoning104

Lake Above - Fire Below105

50 Fan the Flame of a New Beginning106

Fire Above - Wood Below107

51 Shake Rattle and Roll108

Thunder Above - Thunder Below109

52 When There is Nowhere to Go110

Mountain Above - Mountain Below111

53 The Wild Goose Rides the Winds112

Wind Above – Mountain Below113

54 To Seek a Favorable Position114

Thunder Above – Lake Below115

55 The Illumination of Awareness116

Thunder Above - Fire Below117

56 The Ways of the Wanderer118

Fire Above - Mountain Below119

57 Go Gently Like the Wind120

Wind Above - Wind Below121

58 The Animation of Joy122

Lake Above - Lake Below123

59 The Dispersion of Stagnation124

Wind Above - Water Below125

60 The Limitations of the Measure of Time126

Water Above - Lake Below   127
61 The Inner Truth of an Open Heart   128
Wind Above - Lake Below   129
62 The Small Bird Remains in Her Nest   130
Thunder Above - Mountain Below   131
63 The Instability of Coexistence   132
Water Above – Fire Below   133
64 The Fox Crosses the River   134
Fire Above - Water Below   135
The Taoist Principle of Yin and Yang   136
Asking Your Question   137
The Taoist Principle of Eternal Change   138
The Threads of Your Life   144

The Threads of Your Life

The time has come to diverge from all that has been taught
to the child that you have left behind.

Now you seek the way to be who you really are.

You are a thread in the wisdom of the past
as it plunges beyond all that has ever been known.

What you understand in your life, is
the gift of your ancestors.
Your suffering is the thread of their suffering.

Your talents are the gifts of the knowledge
they gained in their lifetime, the migrations
of their choices brought you to where you are.

Now you are the ancestor.
All that you have gained in your lifetime
is wisdom in the thread of those not yet born.

Somehow you have learned
many new ways of being in the world.
Choose carefully as you move into the future,
what you experience is your gift.

Discover the way to homogenize all that you have learned,
into something of value that is great enough,
to weave into the threads of the wisdom of your life.

Do not waste this precious time.

Heaven Thunder Water Mountain
Earth Wind Fire Lake

1	34	5	26	11	9	14	43
25	51	3	27	24	42	21	17
6	40	29	4	7	59	64	47
33	62	39	52	15	53	56	31
12	16	8	23	2	20	35	45
44	32	48	18	46	57	50	28
13	55	63	22	36	37	30	49
10	54	60	41	19	61	38	58

That Which Always Is

Heaven, the dynamic force of yang,
seeks the magnetic force of Yin.
Earth, the sustaining power of Yin supports new growth.
Fire flares up and moves on, always seeking new fuel.
Water always follows the path of least resistance.
Thunder shocks and startles, awakening awareness.
The Mountain always stands firm in stillness.
The Wind always stimulates change.
The Lake supports the Wind to carry the rain.